THE MASTER KEY TO SPEAKING AND WRITING CORRECTLY

DON'T
Say THAT

**A SHORT GUIDE TO
BECOMING THE MASTER OF
YOUR COMMUNICATION**

VALERIE J. PAYTON

motique media

Publishing division of Motique Momentums, LLC

www.danielaGabrielle.com

Copyright © 2014 Valerie J. Payton

www.theliteracystudio.com

ISBN: 1507587651
ISBN-13: 9781507587652

This book is dedicated to

YOU . . .

TABLE OF CONTENTS

THE PARTS OF SPEECH..........5
A Quick Review

EIGHT KEYS TO BECOMING THE

MASTER OF *Your* COMMUNICATION

1 **NOUNS**.....................................7

Common and Proper Nouns • Singular and Plural Nouns
Various Rules for Forming the Plural • Possessive Nouns
Singular Possessive Nouns • Plural Possessive Nouns
Plural Noun or Possessive Noun • Showing Possession with the
Days of the Week and the Months of the Year

2 **VERBS**.....................................19

Action Verbs • State-of-Being Verbs • Using Helping Verbs
Main Verbs • Verb Tenses • Forming the Present Tense of
Verbs • Forming the Past Tense of Verbs • Irregular Verbs in
the Past Tense • Forming the Future Tense of Verbs • Staying
in the Same Verb Tense • Principal Parts of Irregular Verbs
Confusing Verbs • Verbs Confused with Words That Are Not
Verbs

3 ⚷ PRONOUNS..............................43

Replacing Nouns and Antecedents with Pronouns • Singular Pronouns • Plural Pronouns • Using Pronouns and Antecedents in Special Ways • Subject Pronouns • Subject Pronouns Before Action Verbs • Subject Pronouns After State-of-Being Verbs • Subject Pronouns Followed by a Noun Object Pronouns • Object Pronouns After Action Verbs Object Pronouns After Prepositions • Compound Object Pronouns After Prepositions • Pronouns After *Than* and *As* Using Reflexive Pronouns Ending with *–self* or *–selves* Using the Relative Pronouns *Who* and *Whom* • Using *Whoever* and *Whomever* • Possessive Pronouns • Possessive Pronouns Before Nouns • Possessive Pronouns That Stand Alone Using Possessive Pronouns in a Special Way • Possessive Pronouns and Contractions • Indefinite Pronouns • Singular Indefinite Pronouns • Plural Indefinite Pronouns

4 ⚷ SUBJECT & VERB AGREEMENT....69

Singular Subjects • Plural Subjects • The Pronouns *You* and *I* As Subjects • Singular Subjects Ending in *–s* • Plural Subjects Not Ending in *–s* or *–es* • Subject and Verb Agreement with Special Verbs • Using *Is, Are, Was,* and *Were* with Subjects • Using the Pronoun *I* with *Am* and *Was* Using *Has* and *Have* with Subjects • Using *Does* and *Do* with Subjects • Using the Verb *Were* in the Subjunctive Mood Subject and Verb Agreement with the Compound Subject Using the Conjunction *And* in a Compound Subject • Using Compound Subjects with *Or, Either-or,* and *Neither-nor* Subject and Verb Agreement with *Here, There,* and *Where* Using *Here, There,* and *Where* as Contractions

5 ⟜PREPOSITIONS......................91

List of Commonly Used Prepositions • Prepositional Phrases
Object Pronouns after Prepositions • Subject/Verb Agreement
and the Object of the Preposition • Using the Prepositions
Between and *Among* • Prepositions at the End of Sentences

6 ⟜ADJECTIVES..........................101

Adjectives Tell *What Kind, Which One,* and *How Many*
Adjectives before Nouns • Adjectives after Nouns and
Pronouns • Demonstrative Adjectives *This, That, These,* and
Those • Adjective or Pronoun? • Special Adjectives
Proper Nouns as Proper Adjectives • Articles *A, An,* and *The*
Making Comparisons with Adjectives • Comparative Form
Superlative Form • Using *More* and *Most* • Comparative
Form with More • Superlative Form with Most • Irregular
Comparative and Superlative Forms of Adjectives

7 ⟜ADVERBS..............................115

Adverbs Modifying Verbs • Adverbs Modifying Adjectives
Adverbs Modifying Adverbs • What Do Adverbs Tell about
Words They Modify? • Adverbs Not Ending in *–ly* • Using
Adverbs and Adjectives • Making Comparisons with Adverbs
Comparative Form • Superlative Form • Using *Good* and
Well, Bad and *Badly* • Adjectives *Good* and *Bad* • Adverbs
Well and *Badly* • Using *Good* or *Well*

8 ⟜DOUBLE NEGATIVES..........127

Common Negative Words • Contractions with the Negative
Word *Not* • Common Positive Words • Avoiding Double
Negatives

ACKNOWLEDGMENTS

With special thanks:

- To all of the wonderful students I taught at P.S. 133M/The Fred R. Moore School in Harlem. You made teaching such a rewarding experience for me . . . years filled with love, appreciation, good times (and some challenges), and those amazing memories that are forever etched in my heart.
- To the parents, for trusting me to teach your children, and for allowing me to care for them as if they were my own. Your support made it all possible.
- To the most phenomenal principal, Mr. Edward Jackson. You saw something in me and made me know that I was born to teach. I told you I was writing a book, but I am so sorry I did not get a chance to share it with you. I can hear you saying, "Good job Valerie."
- To my mother, Nanine Payton. At a very young age, while spending summers with you in New York, you sparked my interest in the English Language and speaking correctly. I remember asking, "Where is the Empire State Building at?" Your response was, "It's behind the preposition '*at*.'" When I said, "There goes the Empire State Building," you asked, "Where is it going?"
- To my awesome children, Tasean and Shakeerah, for having to come home to a teacher after being in school all day. You endured the corrections, and most of the time you welcomed them with love. Believe me, my grandchildren, Kiarah, Ashanna, TJ, and Jade, were not excluded from grandmommy's occasional corrections.

- To my "First Look" Focus Groups, the family members and friends who honored me and carefully examined my book as "the consumer." Because of you and your awesome feedback, the book is even better than I could have imagined.

Shakeerah Shuford	Meeka Pigford	Tasean Shuford
Donna Conwell	Marilyn Bass	Paris Madison
Alexa Brito	Krisheita Robinson	Brhea Phoenix
Lisa Sharp	Inez Brown	Grace McLean
Donna Hicks Izzard	Mayvis Payne	Keanna Henson

- To my book coach, Daniela-Gabrielle Smallwood. The conference calls, one-on-one sessions, and the powerful tasks assigned were what I needed to complete the ASSIGNMENT. Take a bow for the amazing job you have done with the production of this book, my dream.
- To my webmaster, William Jordan. You patiently waited for your expert touch to solidify this project. You did a fantastic job expressing me and sharing my ideas in an awesome display.
- To Janice Johnson, my friend and public relations ambassador. Let's do it! The world is waiting!
- To my co-author, God. When my mind couldn't figure out what to write or how to present it, You took over.

INTRODUCTION

"Where was you? Where was you? You should have came upstairs with everybody else!"

Two students, late coming back to class after recess, stood in front of the classroom looking at me while an adult reprimanded them for their lateness. The other students sat in their seats with questioning eyes, and those stares were not because the boys were in trouble. I definitely understood what they wanted to know: "Aren't you going to say anything to him? He's not speaking correctly!"

"Ms. Payton, my grandmother said if I correct her one more time . . .!"

"Ms. Payton, we had to correct the substitute teacher so many times yesterday because she kept making mistakes when she was talking."

I did not want to believe what I was hearing, so my first reaction was, "Guys, you can't do that to a teacher!"

One of the students proudly said, "She didn't mind. She thought we were so smart, and she told us it was okay to keep telling her what to say." Was I embarrassed! I desperately hoped that she was not subbing in the school that day. I could not face her.

Later, a newcomer to the school approached me and asked, "Are you Ms. Payton? I had your class yesterday." I began apologizing. She stopped me immediately, smiled, and told me she enjoyed them and learned so much from them.

If you are wondering what is going on with these students, this book will help you understand. As they learned rules and explanations for speaking the English Language correctly, they worked diligently, using them when they spoke and listened to others. They welcomed the challenge and became the "teachers" to all – in school, at home, on the playground, or wherever they went. The PTA president even told me about an encounter he had in the neighborhood's laundromat. He loved it!

Become "The Master of Your Communication." Perfect your speaking and writing skills. Always be in control of your *spoken words* and your *written words.* Never doubt, or wonder, if you are expressing yourself correctly. This book, *DON'T SAY THAT,* is the key you need to unlock the mystery, erase all doubts, and uncover the secrets found in the "Unforgettable Tips."

Allow these pages to speak to you, and through you, as you take a closer look at some simple explanations for language rules in grammar, spelling, punctuation, and word usage. Use them in your everyday conversations, meetings, speeches, at your family gatherings, and even during your interviews. When you speak with great confidence, you will write with the same authority.

Be careful when telling others what to say and how to say it. Some people need to see it and know it for themselves. Give them the opportunity to discover and embrace the "blueprint" for speaking and writing the English Language correctly.

Recommend this straightforward and powerful tool – *DON'T SAY THAT:* A Short Guide to Becoming the Master of Your Communication.

THE PARTS OF SPEECH

A Quick Review

❖ When you put *words* together to *express ideas* in your *speaking* and *writing*, each word has its own function in the sentence. *All* of the *words* you use are *classified* as one of the *eight* "Parts of Speech."

Parts of Speech

Noun	a word that names a person, place, thing, or an idea
Pronoun	a word used to take the place of a noun
Verb	a word that tells about action, or it tells that someone or something is (state of being)
Adjective	a word used to *modify or describe a noun or pronoun
Adverb	a word used to modify or describe an adjective, a verb, or another adverb
Preposition	a word used to show the relationship, or link, of a noun or a pronoun to another word in the sentence
Conjunction	a word which joins words, phrases, and sentences
Interjection	a word that expresses strong feelings or excitement; it is usually followed by an exclamation point.

*To modify a word means to make the meaning or description of the word more definite.

A Closer Look . . .

❖ Wow! Larry spoke highly of our company and dedicated staff.

• Wow!	Interjection
• Larry	Noun
• spoke	Verb
• highly	Adverb
• of	Preposition
• our	Pronoun
• company	Noun
• and	Conjunction
• dedicated	Adjective
• staff	Noun

Try It Yourself!

Tell the Parts of Speech for the underlined words.

1. The organizers carefully planned the best approach.
2. They donated their service to the organization.
3. Yes! Michael and Robert are here.

Answers

1. organizers (noun); carefully (adverb); best (adjective)
2. They (pronoun); donated (verb); to (preposition)
3. Yes! (interjection); and (conjunction); Robert (noun); are (verb)

NOUNS

❖ *Nouns* are words that name a *person, place, thing,* or an *idea.*

If a *noun* names a *particular person, place, thing,* or *idea,* it is a *proper noun.* It must *begin* with a *capital letter.* A *common noun* names a *general person, place, thing,* or *idea,* and it *begins* with a *lowercase letter.*

Persons	Places	Things	Ideas
Susan	New York	January	love
doctor	office	computer	freedom
principal	school	newspaper	intelligence

Some nouns are *singular,* and some are *plural.* When *nouns* are *singular,* they name *one person, place, thing,* or *idea.* If a *noun* is *plural,* it names *more than one person, place, thing,* or *idea.*

Various Rules for Forming the Plural

1a.   Most *nouns* form the *plural* by *adding –s* to the *singular form.*

Singular Nouns	team	computer	governor
Plural Nouns	teams	computers	governors

1b.   When *singular nouns end* with *s, sh, ch, x,* or *z, add –es* to form the *plural.*

Singular Nouns	Plural Nouns
gas	gases
bush	bushes
watch	watches
box	boxes
waltz	waltzes

1c.   When **singular nouns end** in *–y* with a **consonant before it, change** the *–y* to *–i* and **add *–es*** to form the **plural.**

Singular Nouns	lady	company	party
Plural Nouns	ladies	companies	parties

1d.   The **plural** of **most** nouns **ending** in *–f* or *–fe* is formed by **adding *–s*.** However, the plural of **some** nouns **ending** in *–f* or *–fe* is formed by **changing** the *–f* to *v* and **adding *–s*** or *–es*.

Singular Nouns	roof	leaf	wife
Plural Nouns	roofs	leaves	wives

1e.   Some nouns are **plural without** adding *–s* or *–es*. A **letter** or **letters** in the singular noun **change to form the plural.** Therefore, an *–s* or *–es* is **not** needed at the **end** of the word.

Singular Nouns	Plural Nouns
child	children
man	men
criterion	criteria
alumnus	alumni

Incorrect	All the young *mens* played in the football game.
Correct	All the young *men* played in the football game.
Incorrect	The *criterions* for the proposal were announced.
Correct	The *criteria* for the proposal were announced.

1f.   Some *nouns* are the *same* in the *singular* and *plural forms.* The *context of the *sentence* determines whether they are *singular* or *plural*.

- I saw *a deer* in my backyard this morning. *(Singular)*
- There were *many deer* in my backyard this morning. *(Plural)*
- Did you hear the good *news*? Janice got the *job*. *(Singular)*
- I refuse to listen to *all* the bad *news*. *(Plural)*

*context – the words that are used with a certain word or phrase that help to explain its meaning

Unforgettable Tip!

☞ When you see pictures or hear *stories* about *sheep*,
there is always a *shepherd* – a *person* whose job is
to *take care of,* or *tend, sheep.* It doesn't matter
how many sheep there are, we usually see only
ONE shepherd. Remember that *ONE shepherd*
and think, *"Sheep* is always *said* and *written ONE
way ... S-H-E-E-P." Never* put an –s on *sheep,*
even when you are talking about more than one.

- That *sheep was* lost for over an hour.
  *(singular – one sheep; *singular
  verb – was)*
- *Several sheep were* lost for over an hour.
  *(plural – more than one sheep; *plural
  verb – were)*

Incorrect	There were *thirty sheeps* in the field.
Correct	There were *thirty sheep* in the field.

Try It Yourself!

What is the plural noun for each singular noun?

1. half	3. copy	5. delay
2. tax	4. crises	6. crutches

Answers   **Please refer back to the rules in (parentheses) to remind you of
the explanations in "Chapter 1."**

1. halves (1d)	3. copies (1c)	5. delays (1a)
2. taxes (1b)	4. crises (1e)	6. crutches (1b)

**For more information about "singular verbs" and "plural verbs,"
see Chapter 2 – "Verbs."*

Possessive Nouns

➤ *Possessive nouns* are nouns that *show possession* or *ownership*. They *also* show that something or someone *is for*, or *belongs to*, something or someone. An *apostrophe (')* is used *with* the *possessive noun*.

Singular Possessive Nouns

1g.   If the *noun* is *singular*, *add* an *apostrophe* and *an –s   ('s)* for the *possessive* form.

- The *store's parking lot* is full.
  (singular possessive noun – store's; one store possesses a full parking lot.)
- That *building's alarm* works really well.
  (singular possessive noun – building's; one building possesses an alarm.)
- I am sorry that my *friend's name* was not on the guest list.
  (singular possessive noun – friend's; name belongs to one friend.)

Plural Possessive Nouns

1h.   If the *possessive noun* is *plural* and *ends* with an –s, the *apostrophe* always comes *after* the *–s (s')*.

- The *stores' parking lots* are full.
  (plural possessive noun – stores'; full parking lots belong to more than one store.)

- Those ***buildings' alarms*** work really well.
  (plural possessive noun – buildings';
  alarms belong to more than one building.)
- I am sorry my ***friends' names*** were not on
  the guest list.
  (plural possessive noun – friends'; names
  belong to more than one friend.)

1i.   If a ***plural noun*** does ***not end*** with an *–s*, ***add*** an
        apostrophe and ***an –s ('s)*** for the ***possessive*** form.

- There were many ***children's activities***
  included in the program.
  (plural possessive noun – children's;
  activities for the children)
- After the meeting, there was a ***women's***
  discussion.
  (plural possessive noun – women's;
  discussion for the women)
- The ***people's voices*** will be heard at the rally
  tonight.
  (plural possessive noun – people's; voices
  belong to the people.)

A Closer Look . . .

1j.   When a ***plural noun*** refers to ***more than one,*** but it
        does not show possession, only add an *–s* at the ***end***
        of the ***noun, not*** an ***apostrophe*** and ***an –s.***

        Incorrect   I have made many ***mistake's*** in my
                             life.
                             (not possessive; no apostrophe)

Correct	I have made many ***mistakes*** in my life. ***(plural noun – mistakes; more than one mistake)***
Incorrect	The sponsors donated several ***toy's*** to the organization. ***(not possessive; no apostrophe)***
Correct	The sponsors donated several ***toys*** to the organization. ***(plural noun – toys; more than one toy)***

1k.   When a ***singular noun*** should show ***possession*** with an ***apostrophe and an –s***, do ***not*** write it as a ***plural noun***, referring to ***more than one.***

Incorrect	Each ***pageants participant*** must submit a portfolio. ***(not a plural noun; needs an apostrophe before the –s)***
Correct	Each ***pageant's participant*** must submit a portfolio. ***(singular possessive noun – pageant's; participant for the pageant)***
Incorrect	The ***cars engine*** needs to be replaced immediately. ***(not a plural noun; needs an apostrophe before the –s)***
Correct	The ***car's engine*** needs to be replaced immediately. ***(singular possessive noun – car's; engine for the car)***

11.   When showing *possession* with the *days of the week* or the *months of the year*, use an *apostrophe* and *an –s*.

Incorrect	*Yesterdays celebration* will be etched in my heart forever. *(not a plural noun; needs an apostrophe before the –s)*
Correct	*Yesterday's celebration* will be etched in my heart forever. *(singular possessive noun – Yesterday's; celebration belongs to yesterday.)*
Incorrect	Please look at *Mondays article* in the newspaper. *(not a plural noun; needs an apostrophe before the –s)*
Correct	Please look at *Monday's article* in the newspaper. *(singular possessive noun – Monday's; article belongs to Monday.)*

Unforgettable Tips!

☞ Have you ever seen *signs* that say, **"Mens"** and **"Womens"**? I know when you see them again, you're going to quietly shout, **"There shouldn't be an –s on those words. They are already plural – *Men* and *Women.*"** The sign is *probably* trying to *show possession*; therefore an *apostrophe* must be added *before* the –s, **"Men's"** and **"Women's."**

     • My husband went to the *Men's Room* in the restaurant.
        (possessive noun – Men's; room for the men)
     • I went to the *Women's Department* in the store.
        (possessive noun – Women's; department for women)

☞ Be careful on the *first day* of each *year.* Say, **"Happy New Year"** instead of **"Happy New Years."** Remember! You are *talking* about *one year*. If you *want* to use *an –s*, there must be an *apostrophe before* the –s and a *noun following* it: **"Happy New Year's Day!"**

☞ When you have that *special someone* in your life, make sure you *ask*, **"Will you be my Valentine?"** on *February 14th*. *Never* say, **"Will you be my Valentines?"** You *don't want more than one Valentine*! You want that *person* to be your *one* and *only Valentine.*

☞ A question often asked is, **"Do you add only an apostrophe (Jones') or an apostrophe and an –s**

(Jones's) when you show possession with a person's name that ends with an –s?" *Technically,* the *apostrophe* with the *–s ('s) is correct,* because it is a *singular possessive noun,* but *both ways* are *accepted. Say* the word *out loudly,* and *decide* if you are saying it *with* or *without* the *–s after* the *apostrophe. It's your call!!! Whatever* you decide, you *must definitely use* an *apostrophe* to show *possession.*

- Ms. Williams's coat   Ms. Williams' coat
- Charles's chance   Charles' chance

Try It Yourself!

   A. What is the possessive form for all pronouns in parentheses?

   1. I just bought a one *(year)* subscription for the hottest magazine ever.
   2. *(People)* account of the accident varied.
   3. Four *(designers)* handbags were given as grand prizes. Each designer was there.
   4. She was asked out on several dates, but she only accepted my *(friend)* request.
   5. I can't believe the *(children)* performance during the celebration. Magnificent!!

   B. What word should be used to complete each sentence?

   1. My (friends, friend's) and colleagues met me at the restaurant.

2. (Wednesdays, Wednesday's) store hours have been changed.
3. The (representatives, representative's) decided not to listen to them.

Answers   **Please refer back to the rules in (parentheses) to remind you of the explanations in "Chapter 1."**

A.   1.   year's (1l)
     2.   people's (1i)
     3.   designers' (1h)
     4.   friend's (1g)
     5.   children's (1i)

B.   1.   friends (1j)
     2.   Wednesday's (1l)
     3.   representatives (1j)

VERBS

❖ **A *verb* is a word that *tells* about *action,* or it *tells* that *someone* or *something is (state of being).***

Action Verbs

2a.   Some *verbs* tell about *action* that you *can see.* The *movement* is *visible.*

- My brother *moved* all his equipment into the garage.
- During the game, everyone always *screams* at the television.
- They *stood* up as the president entered the room.

2b.   Some *verbs* tell about *action* that you *cannot see.* The *physical movement* is *not seen.*

- The director *thought* of the best actors for the movie.
- Kevin *knows* the quickest route to the theater.
- I *want* the entire family available for the reunion this weekend.

19

State-of-Being Verbs

2c. **State-of-being verbs** are often referred to as **"to be" verbs** because they **tell** that **something is** or **was**. They are **am, is, are, was, were, be, being,** and **been.** They refer to the **condition, situation,** or **position** that something or someone is in **at a specific time.**

- The **shoppers were** on long lines in the store.
  (state-of-being verb – were; telling about the position of the shoppers)
- The store **manager is** aware of the problem.
  (state-of-being verb – is; telling the situation of the manager)
- The **officer was** brave.
  (state-of-being verb – was; telling the condition of the officer)

2d. **State-of-being verbs** are also called **linking verbs** because they **join** the *subject with a **word** or **words** in the *predicate.* The most common **linking verbs are look, appear, become, seem, feel, remain, smell, taste,** and **sound**.

- **Eleanor seems** very **annoyed** with her best friend.
  (linking verb – seems; linking Eleanor with annoyed)

For more information on "subject" and "predicate," see Chapter 4 – "Subject and Verb Agreement."

- The *executives remained calm* during the employees' protest.
  (linking verb – remained; linking executives with calm)
- A *concert sounds* like a *great idea*.
  (linking verb – sounds; linking concert with great idea)

Using Helping Verbs

Sometimes a *verb* can be a *group* of *words*. When *other verbs* are put with a *main verb*, they are called *helping verbs*. *Common helping verbs* are forms of *be (be, am, is, are, was, were, been)*, *have (have, has, had)*, and *do (do, does, did)*.

2e.   The *main verb* is the *last word* in the group, and the *verb* or *verbs* that come *before* it are *helping verbs*.

- Earl *is considered* the best writer in his class.
  (helping verb – is; main verb – considered)
- We *should have remembered* that experience and learned from it.
  (helping verbs – should, have; main verb – remembered)
- They *did promote* him because of his excellent research.
  (helping verb – did; main verb – promote)

2f.   Sometimes another *word* might come *between* the *helping verb* and the *main verb*.

- The sisters *have* always *shared* a love for classical music.
  (helping verb – have; main verb – shared)
- The men in my house *will* never *consent* to a month without sports.
  (helping verb – will; main verb – consent)
- *Does* the noise outside *interfere* with your concentration?
  (helping verb – Does; main verb – interfere)

2g. Some *main verbs end* in *–ing,* and *they* must *always* have a *helping verb before* them.

Incorrect	They *watching* their favorite movie.
Correct	They *are watching* their favorite movie. *(helping verb – are; main verb – watching)*
Incorrect	She *being* very friendly now because she wants my vote.
Correct	She *is being* very friendly now because she wants my vote. *(helping verb – is; main verb – being)*
Incorrect	You *listening* to me?
Correct	*Are* you *listening* to me? *(helping verb – Are; main verb – listening)*

Unforgettable Tips!

- *ALL sentences* must have a *verb*. *Sometimes* a verb is the *only word* in the sentence. I know you are *thinking* that there is *no way* a *sentence* can be just *one word*! Check out these *one-word sentences:*

  - Stop.
  - Look.
  - Listen.

- Are you *wondering*: **"Where is the subject or the noun? Who should 'Stop,' 'Look,' and 'Listen'? The sentence has to be about someone or something."** It is! The *subject* of the sentence is the **"Understood You."** That means that the *subject* is *not written*, *but* it is *understood* that **"You"** are being commanded. **The "You" Power!!**

  - *(You)* stop.
  - *(You)* look.
  - *(You)* listen.

- Remember! *Verbs ending* with *–ing* can *never stand alone* as the only verb in the sentence. They must *ALWAYS* have a *helping verb. HELP is on the way "–ing verbs!!" You are NOT ALONE!!*

  - Diana *is worrying* about her reputation.
  - *Is* he *staying*, or *is* he *leaving?*

Try It Yourself!

A. Find the verbs in the sentences and tell if they are main verbs or helping verbs.

    1. This is not happening right now!
    2. We have spent so many summers at the beach.
    3. Does your group ever win the trophy for the best talent?

B. Find the state-of-being verbs and tell what words are being linked.

    1. This meal tastes extra good today.
    2. She feels excited about the opportunity to work as an intern.
    3. Everything I have done appears to be correct.

Answers **Please refer back to the rules in (parentheses) to remind you of the explanations in "Chapter 2."**

A.   1. MV– happening; HV – is (2f)
    2. MV – spent; HV – have (2e)
    3. MV – win; HV – Does (2f)

B.   1. S-O-B Verb – tastes; linking meal and good (2d)
    2. S-O-B Verb – feels; linking She and excited (2d)
    3. S-O-B Verb – appears; linking Everything and correct (2d)

Verb Tenses

❖ *Verb tenses* **tell about** *time.* **They** *tell* **if the** *action* **or the** *state of being of the verb* **takes place in the** *present, past,* **or the** *future.*

Forming the Present Tense of Verbs

The *present tense* tells about an *action* or a *state of being happening now.*

2h.   Use the **basic form* of the verb if the *subject* is a *plural noun* or the ****pronouns** *I* or *you.* Also use the **state-of-being verb** *are* with *plural nouns* and *pronouns*.

- *The* **clients compliment** the artists on their great work.
  (subject/plural noun – clients; basic form of verb – compliment)
- I *need* your help with this new phone.
  (subject/pronoun – I; basic form of verb – need)
- *You are* so amazing!
  (subject/pronoun – You; state-of-being verb – are)

2i.   *Add* an *–s* or *–es* to the *basic form* of the verb if the *subject* is a *singular noun* or *pronoun.* Also use the **state-of-being verb** *is* if the *subject* is *singular.*

*basic form of the verb – verb written with no added endings
**For more information on "pronouns," see Chapter 3 – "Pronouns."

- The *client compliments* the artists on their great work.
  (subject/singular noun – client; -s added to basic form – compliments)
- *Mary needs* your help with her new phone.
  (subject/singular noun – Mary; -s added to basic form – needs)
- *She is* so amazing!!
  (subject/singular pronoun – She; state-of-being verb – is)

Forming the Past Tense of Verbs

The *past tense* tells about an action or state of being that *happened already* in the *past*.

2j.   To form the *past tense* of most verbs, *add –ed* to the *basic form* or present tense.

- The men *knocked* over the expensive vase during the move.
- Danny *yelled* for help when he realized there was a serious problem.
- All of them *worked* twelve-hour shifts for one month.

2k.   Some verbs *end* with a *silent –e*. *Drop* the *–e* from the verb *before* adding the *–ed* to form the past.

- I *lived* in that neighborhood for twenty-five years.
  (basic form/present tense – live; past tense – lived)

- Her attitude *improved* so much since last year.
  (basic form/present tense – improve; past tense – improved)

21. A *principal part* of a verb is the *past participle*. The *past participle* is *formed* with a *helping verb* and the *past tense* of the verb. *Regular past tense verbs* can *ALWAYS stand alone* as the *main verb*.

  - My sister *(has) introduced* me to some fantastic people.
  - My colleagues *(had) warned* me about the strict rules.
  - I *(have) told* you the same thing, over and over again.
  - Michael *(was) called* for a second interview.

Irregular Verbs in the Past Tense

Irregular verbs form the *past tense* in *special ways*.

2m. *Irregular verbs* form the *past tense* by *changing* a *letter* in the *middle* of the *word,* or by having a *completely different spelling* than the *present tense* of the verb.

  - The attorney *spoke* briefly about the case.
    (past tense – spoke; basic form/present tense – speak)
  - Melvin *wore* his special uniform to greet all the visitors.
    (past tense – wore; basic form/present tense – wear)

- I *wrote* an important speech to uplift their spirits.
  (past tense – wrote; basic form/present tense – write)

2n. A *principal part* of the *irregular past tense verbs* is also the *past participle. Most *irregular past participle verbs* can *NEVER stand alone.* They must be used with *helping verbs* to form the *past tense.*

- The attorney *has spoken* briefly about the case.
  [past participle – (has) spoken]
- Melvin *had worn* his special uniform to greet the visitors.
  [past participle – (had) worn]
- I *have written* an important speech to uplift their spirits.
  [past participle – (have) written]

2o. A *few irregular verbs* are the *same* in the *past tense* and the *past participle.*

- He said that his parents *taught* him to respect his elders.
  (basic form/present tense – teach; past tense – taught)
- He said that his parents *have taught* him to respect his elders.
  [past participle – (have) taught]

**For a list of "Common Irregular Verbs . . . Past Participle Verbs,"
see pages 31 and 32.*

- Denise *said* that several complaints were made about the cost of the event.
  (basic form/present tense – say; past tense – said)
- Denise *has said* that several complaints were made about the cost of the event.
  [past participle – (has) said]

Forming the Future Tense of Verbs

The *future tense* tells about an action or a state of being *happening later* – in the *future*.

2p.   Use the **helping verbs** *will* or *shall* with the *basic form,* or *present tense*, of the verb to *form* the *future tense*.

- The decorators *will meet* at the hotel at 4:00 p.m.
  (future/helping verb– will; basic form/present tense – meet)
- What *shall* I *do* about the phone call I received from my partner?
  (future/helping verb – shall; basic form/present tense – do)

A Closer Look ...

2q.   When speaking and writing, remember to *stay* in the *same verb tense. Avoid beginning* with *one* tense and *switching* to *another* one while *talking* about the *same situation.*

Incorrect	I *traveled* a long distance. I *stop* and *eat* several times. *(past tense – traveled; present tense – stop, eat)*
Correct	I *traveled* a long distance. I *stopped* and *ate* several times. *(past tense – traveled; past tense – stopped, ate)*
Incorrect	Tammy *sees* a great opportunity, and she *was* excited. *(present tense – sees; past tense – was)*
Correct	Tammy *sees* a great opportunity, and she *is* excited. *(present tense – sees; present tense – is)*
Incorrect	The toddler *woke* up and *said* he *is* hungry. *(past tense – woke, said; present tense – is)*
Correct	The toddler *woke* up and *said* he *was* hungry. *(past tense – woke, said; past tense – was)*

Principal Parts of Common Irregular Verbs
Using the Past Participle Correctly

❖ Remember to always use a *helping verb before* the *past participle.*

The *helping verbs* that could be used are *has, have,* and *had* and the various forms of the *verb "to be" – am, is, are, was, were, being,* and *been.*

Present	Past	Past Participle
begin	began	(have) begun
blow	blew	(have) blown
break	broke	(have) broken
bring	brought	(have) brought
choose	chose	(have) chosen
come	came	(have) come
do	did	(have) done
drink	drank	(have) drunk
drive	drove	(have) driven
fall	fell	(have) fallen
fly	flew	(have) flown
freeze	froze	(have) frozen
give	gave	(have) given
go	went	(have) gone
grow	grew	(have) grown
know	knew	(have) known
ride	rode	(have) ridden
ring	rang	(have) rung
rise	rose	(have) risen
run	ran	(have) run
see	saw	*(have) seen
sing	sang	(have sung

ALWAYS use a *helping verb* with the **verb** *seen.*

speak	spoke	(have) spoken
steal	stole	(have) stolen
swim	swam	(have) swum
take	took	(have) taken
throw	threw	(have) thrown
wear	wore	(have) worn
write	wrote	(have) written

Incorrect	I seen him before.
Correct	I saw him before.
Correct	I have seen him before.

Try It Yourself!

A. Complete each sentence with the correct past tense or past participle verb.

1. He should have (run, ran) for president.
2. It wasn't (taken, took) from this office.
3. Beverly has (wore, worn) that outfit twice.
4. I (went, gone) there several times last year.

B. Tell if the sentences are correct or incorrect.

1. I knew I should have blew my hair out.
2. The delivery man rung the bell, but he didn't get an answer.
3. Jake and Ritz have rode on his private jet.

Answers

A. 1. run
   2. taken
   3. worn
   4. went
B. 1. Incorrect (blown)
   2. Incorrect (rang)
   3. Correct

Unforgettable Tip!

- Remember that the *past* is *over,* and *–ed* (*forever done*) is at the *end* of most *past tense verbs.*

  - I *lived* my life *yesterday.* Life *yesterday* is *forever done*!

- The *future* is *not here* yet, but it *will* come. *Will* usually comes *before* the verb. This is an *indicator* that *something* is *before* the future.

  - I *will* live my life *tomorrow.* Life *tomorrow* is *not here* yet.

- That **something** *before* the *future* is the *present*, the *g-i-f-t*!! The *gift is for today, not yesterday and not tomorrow!!* It is *now.* Just keep it *basic*! Always *use* the *basic form* of the *verb.*

  - I *live* my life *today.* Life *today* is *now* … a true *gift*! *Just live it!!!*

- *No matter* how much an *irregular past participle verb wants* to *be* by *itself,* it can *NEVER* stand *alone*! It must *always* have *company* – a *helping verb.* If it *refuses* the *help,* then it can *only be* a *past tense* verb, *not* a *past participle* verb. It can *forget* the *fancy name*!!!

Incorrect	I *done* this before. *(Never alone!)*
Correct	I *have done* this before. *(Take the help.)*
Correct	I *did* this before. *(Go back to the past tense.)*

Incorrect	Liz **sung** the song yesterday. *(Never alone!)*
Correct	Liz **had sung** the song yesterday. *(Take the help.)*
Correct	Liz **sang** the song yesterday. *(Go back to the past tense.)*

Try It Yourself!

A. Choose the correct word(s) to complete each sentence.

1. Larry has (flew, flown) to New York.
2. John (keep, keeps) insisting that they (send, sent) a replacement already.
3. I (see, will see) you when I get there.
4. You (know, knew) what was happening before it happened.
5. Who (drunk, drank) the juice I was saving to have with my dinner?

B. Correct each sentence.

1. I kept myself together as I hear the bad news.
2. Bob had gave his resume to the director.

Answers   **Please refer back to the rules in (parentheses) to remind you of the explanations in "Chapter 2."**

A. 1. flown (2n,)   2. keeps (2i), sent (2m)
     3. will see (2p)   4. knew (2m)
     5. drank (2m)

B. 1. I kept myself together as I **heard** the bad news. (2o)
     2. Bob **had given** his resume to the director.
        Bob **gave** his resume to the director.

Confusing Verbs

❖ Several *pairs* of *verb* are often *confused*. **Always think about the **context* of the *sentence* and the *verb's meaning* to determine which verb should be used.**

2r. **Sit and Set**

❖ *Sit* means **to rest the body in an upright position. *(past tense – sat)***
❖ *Set* means **to put or to place something.**

- *Sit* down and enjoy the show.
  (resting the body)
- Do not *set* the flowers on my desk.
  (placing the flowers)

Incorrect   *Sit* the bags on top of the counter.
Correct   *Set* the bags on top of the counter.
(*The bags need to be placed on the counter.*)

2s. **Can and May**

❖ *Can* means **to be able or capable.**
❖ *May* means **to allow; to permit.**

- Everyone on the team *can* make a difference. (*is able to*)
- You *may not* sign these documents without a witness. (*not allowed*)

*context – the words that are used with a certain word or phrase that help to explain its meaning

Incorrect	Can I borrow your lawn mower?
Correct	May I borrow your lawn mower?
	(I am asking for permission.)

2t. Lie and Lay

- ❖ *Lie* means **to recline; to rest.** *(lying, lain)*
- ❖ *Lay* means **to put or place something on a surface.** *(laying, laid)*

  - He said to *lie* down with the feet elevated.
    (Rest with feet elevated.)
  - *Lay* your clothes on the bed in your room.
    (Place your clothes.)

Incorrect	*Lay* on the beach all day!
Correct	*Lie* on the beach all day!
	(Recline on the beach.)

2u. Bought and Brought

- ❖ *Bought* is the *past tense* and *past participle* of *buy,* and it means **to purchase in exchange for money.**
- ❖ *Brought* is the *past tense* and *past participle* of *bring,* and it means **to come with someone or something to a place; to carry to a certain place.**

  - She *bought* the last pair of shoes in that size.
    (purchased with money)
  - Anna *brought* my favorite dish to our potluck dinner.
    (came with it to the dinner)

Incorrect	This is my umbrella. I **bought** it out of my car.
Correct	This is my umbrella. I **brought** it out of my car.
	(I carried the umbrella from my car.)

2v. *Insure and Ensure

* *Insure* means **to protect against loss of life or property with insurance.**
* *Ensure* means **to make sure or certain that something happens; to make sure something is done.**
    * She **insured** her car with a reputable company.
      (She protected her car with insurance.)
    * He **ensured** me that the entertainer would perform.
      (He made certain the entertainer would perform.)

Incorrect	My boss **insured** us that he would hire her.
Correct	My boss **ensured** us that he would hire her.
	(He would make sure she would be hired.)

*A few say that "insure" and "ensure" are interchangeable, but most prefer to differentiate between the two words.

Verbs Confused with Words That Are Not Verbs

2w. **Affect and Effect**

- ❖ *Affect* is a verb, and it means **to cause to change in some way.**
- ❖ *Effect* is a noun, and it means **the result or outcome of a cause.**

- • Something you told him *affected* his outlook on life.
  (verb – affected; changed outlook)
- • The *effect* of not following directions caused me a job opportunity.
  (noun – effect; the result of not following directions)

Incorrect   The way you speak to people can *effect* them profoundly.

Correct   The way you speak to people can *affect* them profoundly.
  (It can cause a change in them.)

2x. **Accept and Except**

- ❖ *Accept* is a verb, and it means **to receive; to take what is given.**
- ❖ *Except* is used mostly as a preposition, and it means **not including; leaving out.**

- • With my whole heart, I *accept*
  (verb – accept; receive apology)
- • *Except* for Irene, we are all going.
  (preposition – except; not including Irene)

Incorrect	I shouldn't have to *except* this.
Correct	I shouldn't have to *accept* this.
	(I shouldn't have to take this.)

2y. Lost and Loss

❖ *Lost* is the *past tense* and *past participle* of the **verb** *lose,* and it means **to be unable to find; to fail to win; defeated; to be unable to maintain or keep**. It can also be an *adjective* and mean **strayed or missing; not won or likely to be won**.

❖ *Loss* is a *noun* and means **the suffering or damage caused by losing someone or something**.

- My favorite team *lost* and is now eliminated from the competition.
  (verb – lost; failed to win)
- We will join with the organization that is looking for *lost* children.
  (adjective – lost; missing children)
- I am so sorry to hear about your *loss*. You were so close to him.
  (noun – loss; suffering by losing someone)

Incorrect	You are speaking about a *loss* cause.
Correct	You are speaking about a *lost* cause.
	(It is a cause that is not likely to be won.)

Unforgettable Tips!

- Did you pay for it!!! If you *spent* your *money*, use *b-o-u-g-h-t*.

  - I *bought* a new car last year.
    (*spent my money*)
  - I *bought* everything I needed for my house.
    (*spent my money*)
  - I *bought* her a beautiful bracelet for her graduation.
    (*spent my money*)

- Thank goodness that sometimes you *already have the person* or *thing*, and you just have to make sure you *take that someone* or *something with you* when you go to a place. Use *b-r-o-u-g-h-t* this time!

  - I *brought* my husband with me to the car dealership.
    (*took him with me*)
  - I *brought* my old couch with me to the new house.
    (*took it with me*)
  - I *brought* her with me to pick out the bracelet.
    (*took her with me*)

- Let's go **SHOPPING!!!**

  The next time a salesperson walks up to you in a store and says, **"CAN I HELP YOU?"**

Joke with him or her for a minute and say, **"I don't know if you can help me or not. Only you know that. I don't know you like that. How do you feel right now? Do you feel up to it? Are you able or capable?"**

The look on his or her face is probably saying, **"Why did I approach this one!"** because he or she is definitely puzzled.

Now calmly explain yourself: **"I'm not sure if you are able or capable of helping me. I do need help though. You MAY help me! I will allow you. I give you permission!"**

You just helped somebody! You gave a *quick lesson* on when to use *can – to be able or capable,* and when to use *may – to allow or give permission.*

I guarantee you the next time that salesperson approaches someone, he or she will say, **"MAY I HELP YOU?"** because now it is understood that when *asking someone* for *permission*, you must *use* the word *may . . . not can.*

☛ Think about the *last two letters* on the word *lo__ss__ (__so__ sad)* if you are talking or writing about *suffering or damage caused by losing someone or something.* **Because of the __s__adness, *ALWAYS* use the noun** *l-o-__s__-__s__*, and *NEVER* use the **verb** or **adjective** *l-o-s-t.*

Incorrect	That was a devastating *lost*.
Correct	That was a devastating *lo__ss__.*
	(suffering or damage; __so__ __s__ad)

41

Try It Yourself!

Choose the correct word to complete each sentence.

1. Don't do anything that will (effect, affect) your future plans.
2. (Can, May) I give you my opinion?
3. My team had a tremendous (lost, loss). They (loss, lost) the seventh game!
4. I have to (except, accept) how you feel.
5. We (sat, set) and had a heart-to-heart conversation. We (sat, set) our egos aside.
6. (Lay, Lie) and my bed and take a nap.
7. Who's going to (ensure, insure) your jewelry?

Answers   **Please refer back to the rules in (parentheses) to remind you of the explanations in "Chapter 2."**

1. affect (2w)
2. May (2s)
3. loss; lost (2y)
4. accept (2x)
5. sat; set (2r) .
6. Lie (2t)
7. insure (2v)

PRONOUNS

❖ **A pronoun is a word used in place of a noun.**

- *Donna* felt that *Donna's* rights were being violated, so *Donna* spoke up.
- *Donna* felt that *her* rights were being violated, so *she* spoke up.

The *noun* which the *pronoun replaces* is called the **antecedent*. It has to be *stated first* in order for the pronoun to refer to it. The *pronoun* is *used* so that the same *noun*, or *antecedent*, *doesn't* have to be *repeated*. Take a look at the above sentence:

> *Donna* is the *noun*, or *antecedent*. So that it doesn't have to be stated again, *Donna's* is replaced by the **pronoun her**, and *Donna* is replaced by the **pronoun *she*.**

Singular and Plural Pronouns

When you replace a *noun* with a *pronoun*, they *must agree. Always* replace *singular nouns* with *singular pronouns*, and *plural pronouns* must replace *plural nouns*.

*antecedent – a word, phrase, or clause that is replaced by a pronoun in the same sentence or in another sentence

Singular Pronouns

I, my, mine, me,   he, his, him   it, its
you, your, yours,   she, her, hers

- The *boss* gave *his* instructions to the staff before the meeting.
  (singular noun/antecedent – boss; singular pronoun – his)
- *Monica* must reveal what *she* knows about the problem.
  (singular noun/antecedent – Monica; singular pronoun – she)

3a.   A *singular pronoun* must be used to *agree* with *two or more singular nouns/antecedents* that are *joined* by the *conjunctions *or, either-or,* or *neither-nor.*

- *Either Michael or Bill* must submit *his* budget to the committee by noon.
  (singular nouns – Michael, Bill; joined by – either-or;
  singular pronoun – his)
- *Neither Jackie nor Elena* remembered to bring *her* ticket to enter the event.
  (singular nouns – Jackie, Elena; joined by – neither-nor;
  singular pronoun – her)
- The *father or* the *son* has to speak about why we should support *him*.
  (singular nouns – father, son; joined by – or; singular pronoun – him)

conjunctions – words that joins words, phrases, and sentences

Plural Pronouns

we, our, ours, us   you, your, yours
they, their, theirs, them

- The *musicians* entered first, and the singer followed *them.*
  (plural noun/antecedent – musicians; plural pronoun them)
- Give the *students* the opportunity to reach *their* full potential.
  (plural noun/antecedent – students; plural pronoun – their)

3b.   When *two* or *more singular* or *plural nouns* are *joined by* the **conjunction** *and*, use a *plural pronoun* to replace them.

- *Pat and Joshua* prepared for *their* trip to Hawaii.
  (singular nouns – Pat, Joshua; joined by – and; plural pronoun – their)
- The *students, parents, and teachers* participated. All of *them* worked hard.
  (plural nouns – students, parents, teachers; joined by – and; plural pronoun – them)
- Make sure you invite *Michelle and Jeff*. *They* want to attend the affair.
  (plural nouns – Michelle, Jeff; joined by – and; plural pronoun – They)

Using Pronouns and Antecedents in Special Ways

3c.   If *one* of the *antecedents* is *another pronoun*, use
        rules *3a* and *3b* to determine if a *singular* or *plural*
        pronoun is *needed.*

        •   The *ladies and I* support his rights, and *we*
            aren't afraid to stand up.
            *(plural noun – ladies; pronoun – I; joined
            by – and; plural pronoun –we)*

3d.   Sometimes the *antecedent* of a pronoun is *another
        pronoun*.

        •   *You* didn't answer *your* phone when the
            reporter called.
            *(antecedent – pronoun You; pronoun –
            your)*

3e.   Sometimes the *antecedent* that the *pronoun* is
        replacing might *not* be *stated*.

        •   *I* was not aware that the task had to be
            completed in an hour.
            (antecedent – not stated; pronoun – I)
        •   Please call when *you* are outside.
            (antecedent – not stated; pronoun – you)

Unforgettable Tip!

- Do you ever feel that your *conversation* might be a *little boring* because you are *saying* the *same thing* over and over again?

> **Robin** invited me to dinner tonight. **Robin** picked the **restaurant** because the **restaurant** is **Robin's** favorite place to eat, and **Robin** has been eating there all of **Robin's** life. **Robin** and **Robin's** parents own the **restaurant! Robin and Robin's parents** say the **restaurant** has the best food in the city. I'm not going to just take **Robin and Robin's parents'** word! My taste buds will find out for sure if **Robin and Robin's parents** are right!

- Are you tired of repeating the words **Robin, Robin's parents,** and **restaurant?** After you say them the first time, replace them with pronouns. Pronouns to the rescue!!!

> **Robin** invited me to dinner tonight. **She** picked the **restaurant** because **it** is **her** favorite place to eat, and **she** has been eating there all of **her** life. **She** and **her** parents own **it. They** say **it** has the best food in the city. I'm not going to just take **their** word! My taste buds will find out for sure if **they** are right!!

Try It Yourself!

A. Complete each sentence with the correct pronoun(s).

1. My manager and our department were in charge of the fundraiser for the event. (He, They) did a great job.
2. Neither Ken nor Ron was able to motivate (his, their) friend.
3. The grandmother, mother, and daughter were all honored. Did (she, they) get (her, their) special gifts?

B. Indicate which antecedent(s) the underlined pronoun is replacing? If the antecedent is ***not stated,*** put **"NS."**

1. ***You*** weren't supposed to deliver the flowers until after the party.
2. Marcia or Melody will pay for the dinner out of ***her*** company's business account.
3. I didn't receive the right information to answer ***my*** questions.

Answers   **Please refer back to the rules in (parentheses) to remind you of the explanations in "Chapter 3."**

A. 1.   They (3b)
    2.   his (3a)
    3.   they, their (3b)

B. 1.   NS (3e)
    2.   Marcia or Melody (3a)
    3.   I (3d)

Subject Pronouns

❖ The *subject pronouns* are *I, you, he, she, it, we,* and *they. They* are used as the *subjects* of *sentences before action verbs* and *after state-of-being verbs.*

3f.   Use *subject pronouns* as the *subjects* of sentences *before action verbs.*

- *They walked* around the mall for several hours.
  (subject pronoun – They; action verb – walked)
- *I developed* a great method for winning all of our games.
  (subject pronoun – I; action verb – developed)
- *She amazes* me with her photography skills.
  (subject pronoun – She; action verb – amazes)
- *We exercised* in the park every Saturday morning during the summer.
  (subject pronoun – We; action verb – exercised)

3g.   Use *subject pronouns after state-of-being verbs (am, is, are, was, were, be, being, been).* They *refer to* the *subject* of the *sentence.*

- May I speak to *Sarah*? This *is she.*
  (state-of-being verb – is; subject pronoun – she; referring to – Sarah)

- The best *actor* in the movie was *he*.
  (state-of-being verb – was; subject pronoun – he; referring to – actor)
- If you want to know more, talk to the teachers. It was *they* who made it work.
  (state-of-being verb – was; subject pronoun – they; referring to – teachers)
- Even though *I* didn't make the team, it *was I* who cheered the loudest.
  (state-of-being verb – was; subject pronoun – I; referring to – I)

A Closer Look . . .

3h.   Sometimes a *subject pronoun* can be *followed by* a *noun* and *then* a *verb*.

- *We members voted* to dismiss the leadership in our club.
  (subject pronoun – we; noun – members; verb - voted)
- *I, Mr. Jackson, promise* to be fair and listen to everyone.
  (subject pronoun – I; noun – Mr. Jackson; verb – promise)
- *You guys are* simply my favorite performers!
  (subject pronoun – You; noun – guys; verb – are)
- *She, Princess Jade, walks* with humility and pride as she greets the people.
  (subject pronoun – She; noun – Princess Jade; verb – walks)

Unforgettable Tips!

- Oftentimes I hear people say, **"It doesn't sound right. It sounds so awkward."** They don't want to use a subject pronoun after a state-of-being verb. Let us look back at the sentence: *The best actor in the movie was he.* Maybe you want to say, **"The best actor in the movie was him."** You must remember that *he* is referring to, and replacing, *actor.* Quickly think, **"If I turned the sentence around, would I say, 'He was the best actor,' or 'Him was the best actor?'"** The first sentence definitely sounds better! The more you speak and write correctly, the more familiar and easy it becomes.

- Since *nouns don't usually follow subject pronouns*, it can *get* very *tricky* when trying to *figure* out *what pronoun* to use in *front* of a *noun*. Consider another option for this sentence: *We members voted to dismiss the leadership in our club.* Are you *tempted* to *say,* **"Us members voted to dismiss the leadership in our club"**? If you're *not sure, remove* the *noun* that follows the subject pronoun and say the sentence: **"(We, Us) voted to dismiss the leadership in our club."** Of course, you decided that *We* is definitely the *right pronoun* because it is the *subject* of the *sentence*.

Incorrect	*Us girls* celebrated our victory!
Correct	*We girls* celebrated our victory! *(subject pronoun – We; subject/noun – girls)*

Try It Yourself!

Replace the underlined nouns with the correct pronouns.

1. <u>Sam and Vera</u> represented two major cities.
2. The <u>representative</u> didn't want to allow them to speak.
3. It was the <u>representative</u> who thought that there were no problems.
4. <u>Anita, Anna, and I</u> said that everyone was entitled to have an opinion.
5. Our voices would be heard. It was the <u>representative and board members</u> that had to listen.
6. <u>Representative and board members</u> guys have to make better decisions.

Answers   **Please refer back to the rules in (parentheses) to remind you of the explanations in "Chapter 3."**

1. They (3f)
2. he/she (3f)
3. he/she (3g)
4. We (3f)
5. they (3g)
6. You (3h)

Object Pronouns

❖ **The *object pronouns* are *me, you, him, her, it, us,*
and *them*. Use them *after action verbs* and
*prepositions.**

3i.   Use *object pronouns after action verbs.*

- Sammy *invited us* to his birthday party.
  (object pronoun – us; action verb – invited)
- The program director never *called them*
  about the proposal.
  *(object pronoun – them; action verb –
  called)*
- Sylvia *told me* to create a menu that
  everyone can enjoy.
  (object pronoun – me; action verb – told)
- Our colleagues *presented her* with
  wonderful gifts for her new baby.
  *(object pronoun – her; action verb –
  presented)*

3j.   Use *object pronouns after prepositions.*

- If she is not ready by 7:00, we will have to
  leave *without her.*
  *(object pronoun – her; preposition –
  without)*
- The professor spoke *to me* after class.
  (object pronoun – me; preposition – to)

**For more information about prepositions and objects of
prepositions and for a list of commonly used prepositions, see
Chapter 5 – "Prepositions."*

- Although we know this is not *for us*, we will support it.
  (object pronoun – us; preposition – for)
- Danny didn't leave the facility *before them.*
  (object pronoun – them; preposition – before)

Using Compound Object Pronouns After the Preposition

3k.   Sometimes it becomes *confusing* when *using two object pronouns (compound)* or an *object pronoun* and a *noun after* a *preposition. NEVER* use a *subject pronoun.*

Incorrect	This conversation must remain *between you* and *I*.
Correct	This conversation must remain *between you* and *me*.
Incorrect	Make sure you tell them *about Susan* and *she*.
Correct	Make sure you tell them *about Susan* and *her*.
Incorrect	I'm sure he is doing this *for he* and *his family*.
Correct	I'm sure he is doing this *for him* and *his family*.
Incorrect	Be careful what you say *around she and they*.
Correct	Be careful what you say *around her and them*.

Pronouns After Than and As

Should you use a *subject pronoun* or *object pronoun after* the words *than* and *as*?

3l.   A *subject pronoun* is needed *after than* and *as* if the *pronoun* is the *subject* of the *understood verb*, and the *sentence* is *completed* in your *mind*.

       Incorrect   She is more talented *than her*.
       Correct   She is more talented *than she* (*is*).
                           (subject pronoun – she; understood verb – is)
       Incorrect   Harold doesn't seem as committed *as him*.
       Correct   Harold doesn't seem as committed *as he* (*does*).
                           (subject pronoun – he; understood verb – does)

3m.   Occasionally the *thought might end* with a pronoun. When this happens, use an *object pronoun after than.* Think of the sentence as if it has an *understood preposition before* the *object pronoun.*

    •   I would rather be with you *than (with) him.*
       (object pronoun – him; understood preposition – with)
    •   This conversation is needed more for me *than (for) her.*
       (object pronoun – her; understood preposition – for)

Using Reflexive Pronouns

3n.   **Reflexive pronouns** are pronouns that **end** with *–self (singular – myself, yourself, himself, herself, itself)* or *–selves (plural – ourselves, yourselves, themselves).* They **reflect back**, or **refer to**, the **subject** of the **sentence**.

- Don't quote me! *I* am only speaking for *myself*, not the staff.
  (reflexive pronoun – myself; reflecting back to the subject – I)
- *Ed* needs to give credit to **himself** for the success he has achieved.
  (reflexive pronoun – himself; reflecting back to the subject – Ed)
- The angry **neighbors** had to remove **themselves** from the auditorium.
  (reflexive pronoun – themselves; reflecting back to the subject – neighbors)

3o.   **Sometimes** the **reflexive pronoun** is used **incorrectly**. If it does **not refer** back to the **subject**, do **not** use the **reflexive pronoun**. If a **subject** of the **sentence** is **needed, use** a **subject pronoun**. If an **object** is **needed**, use an **object pronoun**.

Incorrect	Maxine and *myself* disagreed.
Correct	Maxine and *I (subject pronoun)* disagreed.
Incorrect	He showed an interest in my product and *myself*.
Correct	He showed an interest in my product and *me (object pronoun)*.

Unforgettable Tips!

- Sometimes you are not sure *which object pronouns* to use when there are *compound objects after* the *preposition* or *after* the *verb*. *When in doubt*, here is an easy way to *figure it out*!!

  - *Take away* the *noun* or the *other pronoun*, and see if the sentence makes sense. **"I bought these suits for Marvin and (he, him)."**
  - Does it sound right saying, **"I bought these suits for he (subject pronoun)"?** You are shaking your head and thinking, **"That's definitely wrong! It makes more sense to say, 'I bought these suits for him (object pronoun).'"** Therefore, the *correct sentence* is, **"I bought these suits for Marvin and him."**

- *Remember! Subjects* and *Objects Don't Mix! NEVER* use a *subject pronoun* and an *object pronoun together.* Of course, the *exceptions* are the **pronouns** *you* and *it* because they are *both subject* and *object pronouns.*

Incorrect	She prepared a delicious meal *for him* and *I*. *(object pronoun – him; subject pronoun – I)*
Correct	She prepared a delicious meal *for him* and *me*. *(object pronoun – him; object pronoun – me)*

Incorrect	*She* and *them* joined the committee. *(subject pronoun – She; object pronoun – them)*
Correct	*She* and *they* joined the committee. *(subject pronoun – she; subject pronoun – they)*

Try It Yourself!

Use a subject or an object pronoun to complete each sentence.

1. (She, Her) and (me, I) are starting our own business.
2. (Us, We) friends will support you with your campaign.
3. Paul and his wife have seats in front of you and (me, I) on the flight.
4. There is no one better than (he, him).
5. It was (I, me) that put the wrong information.
6. I remember what they said about Stacy and (myself, me).
7. Don't ask me if he is better than (them, they).

Answers   **Please refer back to the rules in (parentheses) to remind you of the explanations in "Chapter 3."**

1. She, I (3f)
2. We (3h)
3. me (3j)
4. he (3l)
5. I (3g)
6. me (3j)
7. they (3l)

Using the Relative Pronouns Who and Whom

3p.   **Who** is used when referring to a **noun** or **pronoun** that is the **subject** of the sentence.

- **Who** should receive this prestigious award? **Steve** should receive it.
  (relative pronoun – Who; refers to subject/noun – Steve)
- **Tammy** is the one **who** deserves the job.
  (relative pronoun – who; refers to subject/noun – Tammy)
- We know **who they** are because of the reports we read.
  (relative pronoun – who; refers to subject/pronoun – they)
- It was **I who** paid close attention to details.
  (relative pronoun – who; refers to subject/pronoun– I)

3q.   **Whom** is used when referring to a **noun** or **pronoun** that is the **object** of an **action verb** or the **object** of the **preposition.**

- **Whom** do you think they **chose** as the new president? I think they **chose Ted**.
  (relative pronoun – Whom; refers to noun – Ted; object of verb – chose)
- **Beth**, **whom** I **admire**, granted my wish.
  (relative pronoun – whom; refers to noun – Beth; object of verb – admire)
- **To whom** should I give this important document? Give it **to Sharon**.
  (relative pronoun – whom; refers to noun – Sharon; object of preposition – to)

- I am the young *lady whom* the mayor speaks *about* in the article.
  (relative pronoun – whom; refers to noun – lady; object of preposition – about)

Using Whoever and Whomever

3r. *Whoever* follows the *same rule* as the relative pronoun *who (3p)*. Use it when *referring* to the *subject* that comes *before* the *verb*.

- *Whoever said* that we would not win must be surprised.
  (relative pronoun/subject – whoever; verb – said)
- Sylvia, or *whoever borrowed* my bag, needs to return it today!
  (relative pronoun/subject – whoever; verb – borrowed)

3s. *Whomever* follows the same rule as the relative pronoun *whom (3q)*. Use it when *referring* to the *object*.

- I need to speak *with whomever* is in charge of security.
  (relative pronoun/object – whomever; preposition – with)
- We will *allow whomever* to participate in the celebration.
  (relative pronoun/object – whomever; action verb – allow)

Unforgettable Tips!

- When you are **not sure** if you should use *who* or *whom* in a *question, answer* the *question.* If the *answer* is the *subject* of the sentence, use *who.* If it comes *after* the *action verb* or a *preposition*, use *whom.*

  - *Who* is the director of that film? *Travis Johnson* is the director.
    (The answer is the subject of the sentence – Travis Johnson.)
  - *Who* will show me around this beautiful home? My *son* will show you around.
    (The answer is the subject of the sentence – son.)
  - *Whom* do you choose as a partner? I *choose Jackie.*
    (The answer is the object of the action verb – Jackie.)
  - *With whom* should I meet first? You should meet *with Priscilla.*
    (The answer is the object of the preposition – Priscilla.)

- *Whether* you are using *who* or *whom* in a *question* or *statement*, always *think*, **"If it can be replaced with a subject pronoun (3f, 3g) – he, she, we, or they, use who. If it can be replaced with an object pronoun (3i, 3j) – him, her, us or them, use whom."**

  - Mrs. Johnson is a teacher *who* knows her students. *(She knows her students.)*

- *Who* told you that Dave was interested in going to Paris*? (He told me.)*
- I admire the ladies *who* are focused on their careers. *(They are focused.)*
- Ryan is someone *whom* I can trust with my life. *(I can trust him.)*
- To *whom* should we give the grand prize? *(Give it to her.)*
- Mel and Doris are great agents *whom* we need. *(We need them.)*

Try It Yourself!

Choose the correct relative pronouns to complete the sentences.

1. The dean used the speakers (who, whom) they thought the students respected.
2. Todd is the young man (who, whom) received the most votes.
3. She boldly asked, "To (who, whom) do you thinking you're speaking?"
4. (Who, Whom) gave them permission to use the facility?
5. This ticket is for (whoever, whomever) gets the correct answer.
6. Is someone here (who, whom) wants to challenge the champ?
7. (Whoever, Whomever) decides to stay will be rewarded.

Answers   **Please refer back to the rules in (parentheses) to remind you of the explanations in "Chapter 3."**

1.	whom (3q)	2.	who (3p)	3.	whom (3q)
4.	Who(3p)	5.	whomever (3s)	6.	who (3p)
7.	Whoever (3r)				

Possessive Pronouns

❖ *Possessive pronouns* are used to *show possession* or *ownership*. They *also* show that *something* or *someone is for,* or *belongs to,* something or someone. The *possessive pronouns* are *my, mine, his, her, hers, its, our, ours, their, theirs, your,* and *yours.*

3o.   The *possessive pronouns* used *before nouns* are *my, his, her, its, our, their,* and *your.*

- Come to *my office.*
- This is *our business.*
- Listen to *his proposal.*
- Let them give *their opinions.*
- When is *her appointment?*
- We need *your involvement.*
- I don't like *its color.*

3p.   The *possessive pronouns* that can *stand alone* are *mine, hers, his, ours, theirs* and *yours.* They do *not need* a *noun* to *follow* them. The *noun* is *understood . . . not stated.*

- The car he's driving is not *his.*
  (pronoun – his; understood noun – car)
- I am sure this pocketbook is *yours.*
  (pronoun – yours; pronoun and understood noun – "your" pocketbook)
- All of the dogs were very well-trained.
  Mine won the grand prize.
  (pronoun – Mine; pronoun and understood noun – "My" dog)

Using Possessive Pronouns in a Special Way

3q.   Sometimes *verbs* ending in *–ing function* as *nouns* and are *called gerunds.* Because they are *nouns instead of verbs,* you must use a *possessive pronoun before* them to show *ownership*.

- I would appreciate *your being* on time for the wedding.
  (possessive pronoun – your; functioning as a noun – being)
- *His wanting* to go to the same college touches my heart.
  (possessive pronoun – his; functioning as a noun – wanting)
- *Their talking* during the presentation was disrespectful.
  (possessive pronoun – Their; functioning as a noun – talking)

3r.   If the *verb ending* in *–ing* is *functioning* as a *noun (gerund), never* use an *object pronoun before* it.

Incorrect	I refuse to accept *him acting* like that. *(object pronoun)*
Correct	I refuse to accept *his acting* like that. *(possessive pronoun)*
Incorrect	*Them surprising* me made me cry. *(object pronoun)*
Correct	*Their surprising* me made me cry. *(possessive pronoun)*

Possessive Pronouns and Contractions

3s. Do not confuse the possessive pronouns *its, your, and their* with the **contractions** *it's, you're,* and *they're.*

Possessive Pronoun	The picture is not in *its* proper place.
Contraction	*It's (It is)* the responsibility of the supervisor.
Possessive Pronoun	*Their* friends are meeting them at the mall.
Contraction	*They're (They are)* involved with the plans.
Possessive Pronoun	*Your* time is up!
Contraction	*You're (You are)* in charge of the reservations.

Indefinite Pronouns

An *indefinite pronoun* is a pronoun that does *not* refer to a *specific person* or *thing*. There is *no clear antecedent* because the *person* or *thing* it refers to is *unknown*. It can be *singular* or *plural*.

3t. Some *singular indefinite pronouns* are *each, either, neither, one, everyone, everybody, no one, nobody, anyone, anybody, someone* and *somebody.* Use the **singular possessive pronouns** *his, her,* and *its* with *singular indefinite pronouns*.

- *Someone* left *her* pocketbook in the back seat of the taxi.

(singular indefinite pronoun – Someone; singular possessive pronoun – her)

- *Nobody* knows *his* thoughts about the proposed bill.
(singular indefinite pronoun – Nobody; singular possessive pronoun – his)

3u.   Some *plural indefinite pronouns* are *both, many, few,* and *several.* Use the **plural possessive pronouns** *their* and *our* with *plural indefinite pronouns.*

- *Both* of the nurses gave *their* reports to the doctor.
(plural indefinite pronoun – both; plural possessive pronoun – their)
- *Few* of us knew that *our* president would speak at the convention.
(plural indefinite pronoun – Few; plural possessive pronoun – our)

3v.   *Plural pronouns* should *not* be *used* with *singular indefinite pronouns. Use only singular pronouns.*

Incorrect	*Everyone* gave *their* opinion. *(singular indefinite pronoun – Everyone; plural pronoun – their)*
Correct	*Everyone* gave *his* or *her* opinion. *(singular indefinite pronoun – Everyone; singular pronoun – his, her)*

Unforgettable Tips!

➥ **NEVER** put an *–s* on *mine* when it is a *possessive pronoun*!!!!! Remember that *mines* are *places* where *miners dig*. You *don't want* anyone *digging* in your *mind*, so keep that *–s off* of *mine* when you are speaking or writing about *something* that *belongs* to *you*.

Incorrect	The director says that the leading role is *mines*.
Correct	The director says that the leading role is *mine*.
Incorrect	*Mines* won't be ready before Saturday.
Correct	*Mine* won't be ready before Saturday.

➥ *Contractions* are *words joined* together to make *one word*. Some contractions are *confused* with *possessive pronouns* because they are *homophones (words that sound alike, but are spelled differently and have different meanings)*. *Never* use a *contraction* when you need to *show ownership* or *possession*.

- We really like *you're* new car. (*contraction for* "you are") *(You don't want to say, "We really like you are new car.")*
- We really like *your* new car. (*possessive pronoun*) *(You want to say, "We like the new car that belongs to you.")*

➤ Does the *thing belong* to *someone, or* is it just an *object of someone's affection?* Think about this sentence: **"(My, Me) loving all the children unconditionally has boosted their confidence."** The *subject* of the sentence is the *noun loving (the thing)* which *has boosted* their *confidence.* Therefore, you must use the *possessive pronoun* **"My"** *before* the *noun, not* the *object pronoun* **"Me."**

Incorrect	*Me loving* all the children unconditionally has boosted their confidence.
Correct	*My loving* all the children unconditionally has boosted their confidence.

Try It Yourself!

Choose the correct word(s) to complete each sentence.

1. Neither one admits to (his, their) mistake.
2. I have to take into consideration (its, it's) just not (they're, their) year.
3. (You're, Your) input can make a big difference in my decision.
4. Anybody who doesn't see (his or her, their) counselor today must meet in (your, you're) office tomorrow after class.
5. (Us, Our) spending time together changed my mind about you.

Answers **Please refer back to the rules in (parentheses) to remind you of the explanations in "Chapter 3."**

1. his (3t)   2. it's; their (3s)   3. Your (3s)
4. his or her; your (3t, 3s)   5. Our (3r)

SUBJECT AND VERB AGREEMENT

❖ The *subject* and *verb* of a sentence must *agree.*
They *agree* when they are *both singular,* or *both
of them are plural.*

4a.   If the *subject* is a *singular noun* or *pronoun*
(referring to *one person* or *thing*), *add* an *–s* or *–es*
to the **basic form* of the *verb.*

- That *student ranks* among the top five in the
  country.
  *(singular noun– student; singular
  verb – ranks)*
- *She reaches* unbelievable levels each year.
  *(singular pronoun – She; singular
  verb – reaches)*
- His *contract ends* next month.
  *(singular noun – contract; singular
  verb – ends)*
- *He searches* his heart for the right words to
  say.
  *(singular pronoun – He; singular
  verb – searches)*

4b.   If the *subject* is a *plural noun* or *pronoun*
(referring to more than one person or thing), the
verb must be in its *basic form.*

**basic form of a verb – verb written with no other letters added
to its ending*

- Those **students rank** among the top five in the country.
  (plural noun – students; plural verb/basic form – rank)
- **They reach** unbelievable levels each year.
  (plural pronoun – They; plural verb/basic form – reach)
- Their **contracts end** next month.
  (plural noun – contracts; plural verb/basic form – end)
- **They search** their hearts for the right words to say.
  (plural pronoun – They; plural verb/basic form – search)

4c. If the **subject** is the **pronouns** *you* or *I*, you must also **use** the **basic form** of the **verb.**

- **You deserve** to win a trophy for your great accomplishments.
  (subject/pronoun – you; verb in basic form – deserve)
- **I expect** wonderful things for you in all of your endeavors.
  (subject/pronoun – I; verb in basic form – expect)

A Closer Look . . .

4d. If the **subject** is a **person's name** or a **singular noun** that **ends** with an –*s*, you must **add** an –*s* or –**es** to the **verb.**

- *Charles runs* one of the most profitable businesses in the community.
  (singular noun – Charles; singular verb – runs)
- This *crisis involves* many of the employees from that department.
  (singular noun – crisis; singular verb – involves)
- The *census shows* that five people live there.
  (singular noun – census; singular verb – shows)
- *Ms. Jones watches* and *nourishes* her neighbor's plants.
  (singular noun – Ms. Jones; singular verbs – watches, nourishes)

4e.   If the *subject* is *plural without adding* an *–s* or *–es* to the *noun, do not put* an *–s* or *–es* on the *verb*.

- The *men talk* about ways to get us interested in sports.
  (plural noun – men; plural verb – talk)
- The *children insist* that the adults play every game with them.
  (plural noun – children; plural verb – insist)
- *People admire* so many amazing things in this city.
  (plural noun – People; plural verb – admire)
- My *feet fit* perfectly in the sandals.
  (plural noun – feet; plural verb – fit)

Using Is, Are, Was, and Were with Singular and Plural Subjects

4f.   If the *subject* is *singular*, use the **verbs** *is* or *was.*

- The *coach* of the team *is* concerned about his players' injuries.
  (singular subject – coach; singular verb – is)
- *He was* not sure if they would be ready for the big game.
  (singular subject – He; singular verb – was)

4g.   If the *subject* is *plural* or the **pronoun** *you*, use the **verbs** *are* or *were*.

- The *reports are* false.
  (plural subject – reports; plural verb – are)
- *You were* misinformed about everything.
  (subject/pronoun – You; plural verb – were)

4h.   When the *subject* is the **pronoun** *I*, use the **verbs** *am* or *was*.

- *I am* one of the speakers for the upcoming session.
  (subject/pronoun – I; verb – am)
- *I was* the only person that got a response from the agency.
  (subject/pronoun – I; verb – was)

Using Has and Have with Singular and Plural Subjects

4i.   Always use the **verb *has*** when the ***subject*** is ***singular***.

- *Diane has* a gift for making everyone feel special.
  (singular subject – Diane; singular verb – has)
- My *printer has* no ink.
  (singular subject – printer; singular verb – has)

4j.   Use the **verb *have*** if the ***subject*** is ***plural*** or the **pronouns** *you* and *I*.

- The *teachers have* so many books available on that topic.
  (plural subject – teachers; plural verb – have)
- *You have* enough time to set things up.
  (pronoun – You; plural verb – have)
- *I have* my priorities in order.
  (pronoun – I; plural verb – have)

Using Does and Do with Singular and Plural Subjects

4k.   Use the **verb *does*** when the ***subject*** is ***singular***.

- *Howard does* everything he can to survive.
  (singular subject – Howard; singular verb – does)

- My *assistant does* all of the scheduling for me.
  (singular subject – assistant; singular verb – does)

41. Use the **verb** *do* with a *plural subject* and with the **pronouns** *you* and *I*.

   - The *participants do* quite well when the instructions are clear.
     (plural subject – participants; plural verb – do)
   - *You* never *do* what you are told.
     (pronoun – You; plural verb – do)

A Closer Look . . .

Using the Verb "Were" in the Subjunctive Mood

4m. A *subjunctive mood expresses* an *uncertainty*, a *wish*, or an *unlikely condition*. It *tells* about an *event* that *someone imagines happening* or *anticipates* it *will happen*. In a *subjunctive statement*, the **verb** *were* is *used with* a *singular noun* or *pronoun* and with the **pronoun** *I*. These *words* are *normally used* with the **verb** *was.*

   - *If I were married,* I feel my *outlook* would be very *different.*
     (singular pronoun – I; verb – were; subjunctive mood – If . . . married, outlook . . . different; expresses my imagining it)

- *If Delores were he, nothing* would have been *said.*
  (singular noun – Delores; verb – were; subjunctive mood – If . . . he, nothing . . . said; expresses an unlikely condition)
- I *wish she were here* for the biggest day of my life.
  (singular pronoun – she; verb – were; subjunctive mood – wish she were here; expresses a wish)

Incorrect	*If I was* you, I would do it anyway.
Correct	*If I were you,* I *would do* it *anyway.* *(singular pronoun – I; verb – were; subjunctive mood – If . . . you . . . do anyway; expresses an unlikely condition and anticipates something will happen)*
Incorrect	Juan *wishes* that *he was* a teenager again.
Correct	Juan *wishes* that *he were* a *teenager again.* *(singular pronoun – he; verb – were; subjunctive mood – wishes teenager again; expresses a wish and an unlikely condition)*

Unforgettable Tips!

☞ Remember! If there is an *–s on the subject ... do not put an –s on the verb!* In *most cases*, if there is an *–s* on the *subject*, it is *plural*. Do *not* put an *–s* on the *verb*.

   • Many *parents monitor* what their children watch on television.

☞ Remember! If there is *no –s on the subject ... put an –s on the verb!* In *most cases*, if there is *no –s* on the *subject*, it is *singular*. Therefore, you must *put* an *–s* on the *verb* to make it *singular*.

   • That *parent monitors* what his children watch on television.

☞ **Never** use the **verbs** *is* or *was* with the **pronouns** *you* or *they.*

Incorrect	*You is* responsible for your own actions.
Correct	*You are* responsible for your own actions.
Incorrect	*They was* given enough time to make the necessary changes.
Correct	*They were* given enough time to make the necessary changes.

☞ **The "I" Power!!!** Even though the **pronoun** *I* refers to *only one* person, it *follows* the *rules* of *plural* nouns and pronouns. If the *subject* is *I*, *never* add an *–s* or *–es* to the *verb*.

Incorrect	*I sees* all that you do.
Correct	*I see* all that you do.
Incorrect	*I* always *visits* him during the holidays.
Correct	*I* always *visit* him during the holidays.

Try It Yourself!

Choose the correct word(s) to complete each sentence.

1. Steve (speaks, speak) about the very high standards for the incoming interns.
2. The neighbors (participates, participate) in the annual neighborhood cleanup.
3. I (needs, need) to review the case after you (is, are) done.
4. The men (is, are) in charge of securing the venue for the party.
5. (Does, Do) the CEO know that you (works, work) in the accounting department?
6. The census (shows, show) that over one million people live in the area.
7. Do you think that if Martin (was, were) still here, this would have happened?

Answers **Please refer back to the rules in (parentheses) to remind you of the explanations in "Chapter 4."**

1. speaks (4a)
2. participate (4b)
3. need (4c); are (4g)
4. are (4g)
5. Does (4k); work (4g)
6. shows (4d)
7. were (4m)

Subject and Verb Agreement with a Compound Subject

❖ A *compound subject* has *two* or *more* nouns or pronouns *joined* by the conjunctions *and* or *or*.

Using the Conjunction "and" in a Compound Subject

4n. The *compound subject* is *plural* when the *nouns* or *pronouns* are *connected* by *and*. Use the *plural form (basic form)* of the *verb*. It is also *very important* to use the **verbs** *are* and *were* with a *compound subject*.

- My *friend and* her *coworkers enjoy* traveling together.
  (compound subject – My friend and coworkers; plural verb – enjoy)
- *He and she play* in tennis tournaments around the country.
  (compound subject – He and she; plural verb – play)
- The *employer and employees were* able to come to an agreement.
  (compound subject – employer and employees; plural verb – were)

A Closer Look . . .

4o. Sometimes *two nouns* in the subject are *joined* by *and*, but they are *considered* to be a *singular subject*. Even though they are *two things*, they are *combined* as *one subject*. Therefore, a *singular verb* must be *used*.

- *Drinking and driving is* definitely not good.
  (combined singular subject – Drinking and driving; singular verb – is)
- *Peanut butter and jelly is* my daughter's favorite sandwich.
  (combined singular subject – Peanut butter and jelly; singular verb – is)
- *Right and wrong remains* the same, no matter what we decide.
  (combined singular subject – Right and wrong; singular verb – remains)

4p.　When **singular indefinite pronouns* are *joined* by *and,* they are also *combined as one subject.* A *singular verb* must be used.

- Because they are closing this store, *each* and *everything has* to go.
  (combined singular subject/singular indefinite pronouns – each and everything; singular verb – has)
- *Anything and everything happens* for a reason.
  (combined singular subject/singular indefinite pronouns – Anything and everything; singular verb – happens)
- *Each and everybody speaks* so proudly of what you have done.
  (combined singular subject/singular indefinite pronouns – Each and everybody; singular verb – speaks)

*For information about singular indefinite pronouns, see Chapter 3 – "Pronouns - Singular Indefinite Pronouns" (3t).

Using Compound Subjects with *Or*, *Either-or*, and *Neither-nor*

4q.   If two *singular nouns* or *pronouns* form the *compound subject, joined* by *or, either-or,* or *neither-nor*, the *verb* is also *singular.* Add *–s* or *–es* to the *basic form*.

- *Sally* or *she conducts* the conference call every Monday.
  (singular compound subject – Sally or she; singular verb – conducts)
- *Neither he nor Linda sleeps well during the night.*
  (singular compound subject – he nor Linda; singular verb – sleeps)
- *Either Pamela* or the *producer has* the final word on her new single.
  (singular compound subject – Pamela or producer; singular verb – has)
- I don't believe that *Todd or his company is* ready for this.
  (singular compound subject – Todd or company; singular verb – is)

4r.   If *two plural nouns* or *pronouns* form the *plural compound subject, joined* by *or, either-or,* or *neither-nor,* the *verb* is *plural (basic form)*.

- *Either* the teenage *boys or* the young *men lead* the meeting every night.
  (plural compound subject – boys or men; plural verb – lead)

- *Neither* the *flyers nor* the *posters appeal* to us.
  (plural compound subject – flyers or posters; plural verb – appeal)
- The *risks or challenges determine* how I move forward.
  (plural compound subject – risks or challenges; plural verb – determine)
- *Neither* the *radio stations nor television networks predict* the answers.
  (plural compound subject – radio stations nor television networks; plural verb – predict)

4s. When the *compound subject* has both a *singular* and a *plural subject*, the *verb* must *agree* with the *word closer* to it.

- *Neither* the *owner nor* the *representatives understand* the new contract.
  (representatives – plural noun; closer to plural verb – understand)
- *Neither* the *representatives nor* the *owner understands* the new contract.
  (owner – singular noun; closer to singular verb – understands)
- My *brother or* my *friends* always *come* when I need help.
  (friends – plural noun; closer to plural verb – come)
- My *friends or* my *brother* always *comes* when I need help.
  (brother – singular noun; closer to singular verb – comes)

Unforgettable Tips!

➤ Remember in *MARRIAGE*: *Two become one!*
Some things and some people are one, no matter
what! They have their own *separate identities*, but
they stand together as *ONE*! Even though *some
compound subjects (two or more)* are *joined* by the
conjunction *and*, they function as *single.*
Remember to always think of them as *singular* and
put that *–s* on the *verb*.

- *Spaghetti and meatballs wins* as a favorite
  meal around my house.
- *Cake and ice cream shows* up at the top of
  his list of favorite desserts.

➤ *Don't let* that little word *"or" fool you*! It is
powerful when it comes to *joining words* together.
Pay attention to the *word closer* to the *verb*,
because that's the **word** *"or"* gives the *power* to
determine if the *verb* will be *singular* or *plural.*

- *Are* the *customers* or the salesperson right
  about the price?
  *(word closer to verb – customers – plural;
  plural verb – are)*
- I don't think the customer or the *salesperson
  is* right about the price.
  *(word closer to verb – salesperson–
  singular; singular verb – is)*

Try It Yourself!

Choose the correct word to complete each sentence.

1. Anybody and everybody (was, were) at the movie premiere.
2. Before they leave, Michael and Robert (bids, bid) a fond farewell to everyone.
3. Neither my daughter nor my sons (decides, decide) what to do with the property.
4. Do you know if either the train or the bus (stop, stops) near the arena?
5. The ups and downs of this business (scare, scares) me.
6. I am not sure if his siblings or Richard (is, are) responsible for this.

Answers   **Please refer back to the rules in (parentheses) to remind you of the explanations in "Chapter 4."**

1. was (4p)
2. bid (4n)
3. decide (4s)
4. stops (4q)
5. scares (4o)
6. is (4s)

Subject and Verb Agreement with Here, There, and Where

❖ If the *subject* comes *after here, there,* or *where,* it must *agree* with the *verb* that *comes before* it. Determine if the *subject* is *singular* or *plural,* and then *make* the *verb agree.*

4t. *Singular subjects* must have *singular verbs.*

- Here *is* a very good *suggestion.*
  (singular subject – suggestion; singular verb – is)
- Here *stands* the *statue* of a powerful leader.
  (singular subject – statue; singular verb – stands)
- There *was* a *delay* on my departing flight.
  (singular subject – delay; singular verb – was)
- There *has been* a crucial *decision* made about the funding.
  (singular subject – decision; singular verb – has 'been')
- Where *does he put* the excess materials?
  (singular subject – he; singular verb – does 'put')

4u. *Plural subjects* must have *plural verbs.*

- Here *are* some very good *suggestions.*
  (plural subject – suggestions; plural verb – are)
- Here *stand* the *statues* of powerful leaders.
  (plural subject – statues; plural verb – stand)

- There *were delays* on all departing flights.
  (plural subject – delays; plural verbs – were)
- There *have been* crucial *decisions* made about the funding.
  (plural subject – decisions; plural verb – have 'been')
- Where *do they put* the excess materials?
  (plural subject – they; plural verb – do 'put')

Incorrect	There *need* to be another *cook* in the kitchen.
Correct	There *needs* to be another *cook* in the kitchen. *(singular subject – cook; singular verb – needs)*
Incorrect	Where *was* the *promoters* when the event started?
Correct	Where *were* the *promoters* when the event started? *(plural subject – promoters; plural verb – were)*
Incorrect	Here *lie everything* you need for your trip.
Correct	Here *lies everything* you need for your trip. *(singular subject – everything; singular verb – lies)*

Using Here, There, and Where with Contractions

4v.   If *here, there,* and *where* are written as
        contractions with the *verb is*, follow the *same rules*
        for *singular subject* and *verb agreement*. If the
        subject is *plural*, do *not* use the *contraction*.

- *Here's (Here is)* my *assignment.*
  *(singular subject – assignment; singular
  verb – is)*
- Here *are* my *assignments.*
  *(plural subject – assignments; plural
  verb – are)*
- *There's (There is)* a *seat* available.
  (singular subject – seat; singular verb – is)
- There *are* many *seats* available.
  (plural subject – seats; plural verb – are)
- *Where's (Where is)* the *mistake* you found?
  *(singular subject – mistake; singular
  verb – is)*
- Where *are* the *mistakes* you found?
  *(plural subject – mistakes; plural
  verb – are)*

Incorrect   *There's* the *boxes* for your storage items.
                *(plural subject – boxes; singular verb –
                is)*
Correct   *There are* the *boxes* for your storage
                items.
                *(plural subject – boxes; plural verb –
                are)*

4w.   When *or, either-or, neither-nor* are used with
        here's, *there's* and *where's*, the *singular noun* in
        the compound subject must be *closer* to the
        contraction.

- *There's (There is) neither a train nor taxis*
  available tonight.
  (compound subject – train nor taxis;
  singular noun – train;
  closer to the verb – is)
- *Here's (Here is) either* the *solution or* more
  problems.
  (compound subject – solution or problems;
  singular noun – solution;
  closer to the verb – is)
- *Where's (Where is)* the nearest *mall or* the
  closest *stores* with the best shoes?
  (compound subject – mall or stores;
  singular noun – mall; closer to the verb –
  is)

Unforgettable Tip!

☞ *Here ... There ... Where!* Even though many
sentences begin with these words, you have to
remember, they are *NEVER subjects* of *sentences.*
It *sometimes* becomes *confusing* to decide whether
to use the *singular* or *plural* form of the *verb.*
When you're *not sure*, just simply *ask* yourself,
"Who or what?" *before here, there* and *where* to
find the *subject.*

- Here (is, are) enough food to feed everyone
  who comes.
  *(Who or what is/are here? The food is
  here.)*
  Food is the *subject,* and it's *singular.*
  Use the singular **verb *is*.**
  Here *is* enough *food* to feed everyone who
  comes.
- There (was, were) new skates for the entire
  team.
  *(Who or what was/were there? Skates were
  there.)*
  Skates is the *subject,* and it is *plural.*
  Use the plural **verb *were*.**
  There *were* new *skates* for the entire team.

Try It Yourself!

A. Indicate if each sentence is correct or incorrect.

1. Where's the documents you said you had for me?
2. There's someone coming to join me for dinner tonight.
3. Here's Anthony and Terry.
4. There's neither books available nor anyone to answer my questions.

B. Complete each sentence with the correct verb.

1. Where (do, does) these things go?
2. (There's, There are) neither accurate information nor great workshops planned for the event.
3. Here (is, are) the computers that need to be repaired.
4. There (seem, seems) to be a serious discussion with the family.

Answers **Please refer back to the rules in (parentheses) to remind you of the explanations in "Chapter 4."**

A. 1. Incorrect (4v)
   2. Correct (4v)
   3. Incorrect (4v)
   4. Incorrect (4w)

B. 1. do (4u)
   2. There's (4w)
   3. are (4u))
   4. seems (4t)

PREPOSITIONS

❖ **A preposition is a word used to show the** *relationship,* **or** *link,* **of a** *noun* **or a** *pronoun* **to** *another word* **in the sentence.**

In these sentences, the ***prepositions*** show the ***link,*** or *relationship,* between the ***laptop*** and ***desk.***

- My ***laptop*** is ***on*** my ***desk.***
- My ***laptop*** is ***near*** my ***desk.***
- My ***laptop*** is ***beside*** my ***desk.***

List of Commonly Used Prepositions.

about	before	down	of	to
above	behind	during	off	toward
across	below	for	on	under
after	beneath	from	onto	underneath
against	beside	in	out	until
along	between	inside	outside	up
among	beyond	into	over	upon
around	but (except)	like	past	with
at	by	near	through	without

- I found my **keys between** the **seats**.
  (preposition – between; showing relationship – keys and seats)
- Please put the **money in** the **bank** on the way home.
  (preposition – in; showing relationship – money and bank)
- **She** exercised **on** the **treadmill** for thirty minutes.
  (preposition – on; showing relationship – She and treadmill)
- **After** the **holidays**, we will begin our **rehearsals** for the play.
  (preposition – after; showing relationship – holidays and rehearsals)
- When **you** come to the game, sit **behind** the home team's **bench**.
  (preposition – behind; showing relationship – you and bench)
- Who left these **boxes in** my **office**?
  (preposition – in; showing relationship – boxes and office)
- The **firefighters** went **up** the **ladder** to rescue the family.
  (preposition – up; showing relationship – firefighters and ladder)

Prepositional Phrases

❖ A *prepositional phrase* is a group of words that **begins** with a *preposition* and **ends** with the *object of* the *preposition*, which is a *noun* or *pronoun*.

5a.　Take a look at the ***prepositional phrases*** from the ***previous sentences***:

- *on* my ***desk (preposition – on; object/noun – desk)***
- *near* my ***desk (preposition – near; object/noun – desk)***
- *beside* my ***desk (preposition – beside; object/noun – desk)***

5b.　Sometimes a ***preposition*** can have ***more than one object*** in a phrase.

- The coats are ***for Sarah and*** her ***family.*** ***(preposition – for; objects – Sarah, family)***
- The entire community rallied ***behind Mark, Shelby*** and ***Anthony.*** ***(preposition – behind; objects – Mark, Shelby, Anthony)***
- I function better ***during*** the ***winter*** and ***fall.*** Summer is not my "friend." ***(preposition – during; objects – winter, fall)***

5c.　Always remember to use ***object pronouns (me, you, him, her, it, us, and them) after prepositions.***

- We sat patiently and waited ***for you.*** ***(preposition – for; object pronoun – you)***

- *Without him* and *her*, I don't know what I would do.
  (preposition – without; object pronouns – him, her)
- The producer of the show sent a special invitation *to me*.
  (preposition – to; object pronoun – me)

Subject/Verb Agreement and the Object of the Preposition

5d.　When there is a *prepositional phrase* in a sentence, the *verb* must *agree* with the *subject* of the *sentence, not* the *object* of the *preposition.* The *subject* is *never in* the *prepositional phrase.* It is *usually right before* the *preposition.* If the *subject* is *singular, add –s* to the **basic form* of the *verb,* or use the **verbs** *is, was, has,* or *does.* If the *subject* is *plural* use the *basic form* of the *verb,* or *use* the **verbs** *are, were, have,* or *do.*

- This *collection* of *books is* not for sale.
  (plural object – books; singular subject – collection; singular verb – is)
- The *communities* in that *town* always *support* our charity.
  (singular object – town; plural subject – communities; plural verb – support)
- *Roy*, like his *friends*, *celebrates* twenty-five great years here.
  (plural object – friends; singular subject – Roy; singular verb – celebrates)

*basic form of the verb – verb without a suffix, anything added at the end of the verb.

A Closer Look . . .

Using the Prepositions Between and Among

5e.   There is a *major difference* in the *prepositions between* and *among*. *Between* is used when *speaking* about *two persons, things,* or *groups*. *Among* is used **when** *speaking* of *three* or *more.*

- I need to make a decision *between* the *two builders.*
  (preposition – between; speaking about – two builders)
- They must keep the agreement *between* the *sponsors* and *us*.
  (preposition – between; speaking about – sponsors and us)
- All of our investments were divided *among* the *three companies*.
  (preposition – among; speaking about – three companies)
- He moved quickly *among* the *people* on the crowded platform.
  (preposition – among; speaking about – people)

Incorrect	They distributed the work *between all* the *workers*.
Correct	They distributed the work *among all* the *workers*.
	(among – speaking about three or more – all workers)

Incorrect	True friendship is forever ***between*** the ***four friends.***
Correct	True friendship is forever ***among*** the ***four friends.*** ***(among – speaking about three or more – four friends)***

Prepositions at the End of Sentences

5f.   **MYTH! OPINION!** There is a lot to be said about ***ending*** a ***sentence*** with a ***preposition. Some*** say it is a ***rule*** for ***Latin grammar, not English grammar. Others*** have actually ***called*** it a ***superstition.*** Even though ***I*** am in ***agreement*** with those who say, **"Avoid ending a sentence with a preposition,"** it is acceptable. Here are some ***ways to avoid*** it:

- Where are they ***at***? Where are they? ***(Drop the preposition from the end of the sentence, and you still have a good sentence.)***
- This is the exact bench we sat ***on***. This is the exact bench ***on which*** we sat. ***(Take the preposition from the end and put it in the middle of the sentence with the word*** "which" ***following it.*** "Which" ***is a very popular word to use after the preposition when it is taken from the end of the sentence.)***

- Do you know that's my mother you're talking *to*? Do you know that's my mother *to whom* you are talking?
  (Move "to" to the middle, followed by the word "whom." "Whom" is also very popular to use when you take the preposition from the end.)
- What did you do that *for*? *Why* did you do that?
  (Sometimes by dropping the preposition "for" and changing a word, "What" to "Why," the new sentence does not lose the meaning of what is being said.)

Unforgettable Tip!

➡ *Sometimes* in *life* when you are *confused*, the best way to *stop* the *confusion* is to *get rid* of what is *causing it.* A lot of times you *don't know what verb* to use in a sentence because *you want* to use a *prepositional phrase* also. *Stop* the *confusion*! *Get rid* of the *cause* of the *problem,* the *prepositional phrase. You* want to *say,* "An adequate supply of vitamins are needed daily." Then you start *thinking,* "Wait a minute! Wait a minute! Should it be 'are' or 'is?'" *Break it down . . .*

- What is the *prepositional phrase*? (*of vitamins)*
- What is the *object* of the *preposition*? Is it *singular* or *plural*? *(object – vitamins; plural)*
- What is the *subject* of the sentence? Is it *singular* or *plural*? *(subject – supply; singular)*
- *Remove* the *confusing part*, the *prepositional phrase*, and say the sentence. *[An adequate supply (are, is) needed daily.]*
- Remind yourself that the *verb* must *always agree* with the *subject* of the sentence, *not* the *object* of the *preposition*.
- You have discovered that the **singular verb** *is* is needed to *agree* with the **singular subject** *supply, not* with the word *vitamins,* which is the *object* of the *preposition.*
- Put your prepositional phrase back in the sentence and say it: **"An adequate supply of vitamins is needed daily."** *That's it!!*

Try *It Yourself!*

Choose the correct word(s) to complete each sentence.

1. I know it was done especially for (he, him) and his wife.
2. Is the professional actor rehearsing with you and (I, me) or Larry and (she, her)?
3. The expertise (between, among) all of them is priceless.
4. Knowledge of the rules (is, are) mandatory for the participants.
5. The ambulance, with its siren and flashing lights, (scare, scares) the toddlers.
6. Mistakes in grammar (cause, causes) problems in communication.
7. Please keep this secret (between, among) you and (I, me).

Answers   **Please refer back to the rules in (parentheses) to remind you of the explanations in "Chapter 5."**

1. him (5c)
2. me; her (5b, 5c)
3. among (5e)
4. is (5d)
5. scares (5d)
6. cause (5d)
7. between (5e); me (5b, 5c)

ADJECTIVES

❖ **An *adjective* is a word used to *modify* or *describe* a *noun* or *pronoun*. It can tell *what kind, which one*, or *how many* about the word it modifies.**

What Kind	Which One	How Many
red scarf	*that* desk	*seven* plants
beautiful day	*those* files	*some* men
dedicated employee	the *other* one	*several* books

- Taylor is a *dedicated* employee.
  (kind of employee – dedicated)
- Please review *those* files and give a report.
  (which files – those)

6a.   Some *adjectives* come *before* the *nouns* they modify.

- I found myself in an *uncomfortable position* when I changed jobs.
  (adjective - uncomfortable; noun – position)
- John had *many opportunities* to get it right.
  (adjective – many; noun – opportunities)
- Please help her get started with the *new website*.
  (adjective – new; noun – website)

*To modify a word means to make the meaning or description of the word more definite.

6b.   Some *adjectives* come *after* the *nouns* or
       pronouns they modify.

- *She* is *successful* in everything she does.
  (adjective – successful; pronoun – she)
- *She* is *successful* in everything she does.
  (adjective – successful; pronoun – she)
- The *pilot*, *focused* and *determined, passed
  the test for his license.
  (adjectives – focused, determined; noun –
  pilot)
- *They* were *fantastic* in the starring roles.
  (adjective – fantastic; pronoun – They)

Demonstrative Adjectives

6c.   *Demonstrative adjectives* are *this, that, these* and
       those. They point out *specific things*. Use *this* and
       that to modify *singular nouns*. Use *these* and *those*
       to modify *plural nouns*.

- I am going to use *this frame* for the picture.
  (singular noun – frame; singular adjective
  – this)
- *That sweater* has the best price.
  (singular noun – sweater; singular
  adjective – that)
- All of *these papers* have to be shredded.
  (plural noun – papers; plural adjective –
  these)
- *Those wallets* are on sale.
  (plural noun – wallets; plural adjective –
  Those)

*Sometimes more than one adjective can be used to modify or
describe the same noun.

6d. ***Demonstrative adjectives*** sometimes modify the
singular nouns *kind* and *sort*, so use *this* and *that*.
Use *these* and *those* with *kinds* and *sorts* because
they are *plural.*

- ***That kind*** of behavior will not be tolerated.
  (singular demonstrative adjective – That;
  singular noun – kind)
- Did you know ***those sorts*** of plants need lots
  of care?
  (plural demonstrative adjective – those;
  plural noun – sorts)

Incorrect	***These kind*** of apartments are reasonable. *(plural demonstrative adjective – These; singular noun – kind)*
Correct	***These kinds*** of apartments are reasonable. *(plural demonstrative adjective – These; plural noun – kinds)*

Adjective or Pronoun?

6e. A ***demonstrative word*** can be used as an ***adjective***
or a ***pronoun*** in a sentence. When it tells ***which one***
and is ***followed*** by the ***noun*** that it ***modifies***, it is an
adjective. If it ***takes*** the ***place*** of a ***noun***, it is a
pronoun.

Adjective	***These papers*** should be filed away first. *(demonstrative adjective – These; modifies noun – papers; tells – which papers)*

Pronoun	*These* should be filed away. *(demonstrative pronoun – These;* *replaces the noun – papers)*
Adjective	Did you hear *that noise*? *(demonstrative adjective – that;* *modifies noun – noise; That tells* *which noise.)*
Pronoun	Did you hear *that*? *(demonstrative pronoun – that;* *replace the noun – noise)*

Using Special Adjectives

6f.   *Proper adjectives* are *special adjectives* because
they are *proper nouns modifying*, or describing,
another noun. Like proper nouns, they *begin* with
capital letters.

- The Empire State Building is a *New York*
  landmark.
  (proper noun as a proper adjective – New
  York; modifying – landmark)
- We are invited to *Thanksgiving dinner* at
  Larry's house.
  (proper noun as a proper adjective –
  Thanksgiving; modifying – dinner)

6g.   Some *proper adjectives* are formed by adding
special endings (-n, -ese) to *proper nouns*.

- We are going to my favorite *Japanese*
  restaurant.
  (proper noun – Japan; proper adjective –
  Japanese; modifying – restaurant)

- Georgia was an original *American colony.*
  (proper noun – America; proper adjective –
  American; modifying – colony)

Articles

6h.   There are *three special adjectives* called *articles*
      that *modify nouns.* They are *a, an,* and *the*.

- *A* very important *decision* made history
  today.
  (article – A; modifies noun – decision)
- You have to put forth *an effort.*
  (article – an; modifies noun – effort)
- *The officer* issued tickets to the cars parked
  illegally.
  (article – The; modifies noun – officer)

6i.   Remember to always *use* the article *an before* a
      noun that *begins* with a *vowel* or a *vowel sound*.

an opportunity	*an* island
an umbrella	*an* heiress
an hour	*an* honest person

Incorrect	It is *a honor* to be included on your cabinet.
Correct	It is *an honor* to be included on your cabinet.
Incorrect	He is a father to me and *a uncle* to many.
Correct	He is a father to me and *an uncle* to many.

Unforgettable Tips!

☛ *Never* use the **pronoun** *them* as an *adjective before* a *noun*. A *noun* should *not follow* the word *them* because *them* is a *pronoun* that *replaces* a *noun*.

Incorrect	***Them donuts*** are for everyone at the workshop. *(Pronoun)*
Correct	***These donuts*** are for everyone in the workshop. *(Adjective)* *(adjective – These; modifies the noun – donuts)*
Incorrect	Jim invested in ***them stocks*** last year. *(Pronoun)*
Correct	Jim invested in ***those stocks*** last year. *(Adjective)* *(adjective – those; modifies the noun – stocks)*

☛ *Never* use *here* or *there* with *this, that, these,* and *those. Only* an *adjective* is needed.

Incorrect	***This here*** magazine has some very interesting articles.
Correct	***This*** magazine has some very interesting articles.
Incorrect	They are buying ***those there*** materials for the exhibits.
Correct	They are buying ***those*** materials for the exhibits.

☛ *Do not confuse* **"an"** and **"and."** The **article** *an* is used *before* a *singular noun* that *begins* with a *vowel* or *vowel sound*. The **conjunction** *and* is used to *join two or more words*, *phrases,* or *sentences*. Think about the last letter **"d"** on the word *a-n-d*, and remember *double* means *composed of two parts or members.* If you are *talking* or *writing* about *two* or *more* persons or things, *double* up and *join* them with the word *and.*

Incorrect	My *family an I* participated in the marathon.
Correct	My *family and I* participated in the marathon.
	(conjunction – and; joining family and I)
Incorrect	Visit my page *an* let me know what you think.
Correct	Visit my page *and* let me know what you think.
	(conjunction – and; joining "Visit my page" and ". . . let me know what you think.")

Try It Yourself!

A. Choose the best word to complete each sentence.

1. The young ladies prefer to wear (these, them) beautiful red gowns.
2. I had (a, an) interview last week.
3. (That, Those) sorts of things happen all the time.

B. Is the underlined word an adjective or pronoun?

1. **Those** are for the holidays. Do not touch them.
2. **That** shouldn't be considered a dilemma.
3. **This** information needs be deleted from you profile.

C. Which adjectives describe the underlined nouns?

1. Sarah, with her beautiful **personality**, was chosen as Ms. Congeniality.
2. The **display** that we used for our project was remarkable.
3. Our **relative**, bold and obnoxious, made a ridiculous comment.

Answers   Please refer back to the rules in (parentheses) to remind you of the explanations in "Chapter 6."

A.   1.   these (6c)
     2.   an (6i)
     3.   Those (6d)

B.   1.   Pronoun (6e)
     2.   Pronoun (6e)
     3.   Adjective (6e)

C.   1.   beautiful (6a)
     2.   remarkable (6b)
     3.   bold; obnoxious (6b)

Making Comparisons with Adjectives

❖ **Use the *comparative form* of an adjective to compare *two nouns* or *pronouns*. Use the *superlative form* to *compare three* or *more*.**

6d.   For the *comparative* form, *add –er* to *most adjectives*.

- The *manager's office* is *larger* than the *supervisor's office*.
  (adjective – larger; comparing manager's office and supervisor's office)
- The *speakers* in *my car* are *louder* than the ones in my *friend's car*.
  (adjective- louder; comparing speakers in my car and my friend's car)
- *Today* is *colder* than it was *yesterday*.
  (adjective – colder; comparing today and yesterday)
- Deliver the *prettier* arrangement of the *two*.
  (adjective – prettier; comparing two arrangements)

6e.   For the *superlative* form, *add –est* to *most adjectives*.

- The *manager's office* is the *largest* of the *three offices*.
  (adjective – largest; comparing three offices)
- Out of *all* of my *friends, Jeff's speakers* are the *loudest*.
  (adjective – loudest; comparing the speakers in all friends' cars)

- Today is the *coldest* day of the week.
  (adjective – coldest; comparing all the days of the week)
- Deliver the *prettiest* flowers in the *store.*
  (adjective – prettiest; comparing all the flowers in the store)

Using More and Most

Some *adjectives* have *three* or *more syllables* or a *suffix* at the end of the word. *Instead* of adding *–er* or *–est* when *comparing, use* the words *more* and *most before* the *adjective.*

6f.   For the *comparative form*, add *more before* the *adjective* to compare *two.*

- That *white suit* is *more beautiful* than the *black one.*
  (comparative form – more beautiful; comparing – white suit and black suit)
- *Out of the two of them, Sam* is *more worried* about the situation than *Tom* is.
  (comparative form – more worried; comparing – Sam and Tom)
- What she did *this time* is *more ridiculous* than what she did *before.*
  (comparative form – more ridiculous; comparing – this time and before)
- The *more popular event* of the *two* is the *concert* on Saturday.
  (comparative form – more popular; comparing – one event and the concert)

6g.   For the ***superlative form***, use ***most before*** the ***adjective*** to compare ***three or more***.

- That ***white suit*** is the ***most beautiful*** of ***all*** your ***suits.***
  (superlative form – most beautiful; comparing all the suits)
- ***Out of all the siblings, Sam*** is the ***most worried*** about the situation.
  (superlative form – most worried; comparing all the siblings)
- What she did ***this time*** is the ***most ridiculous*** thing she has ever done.
  (superlative form – most ridiculous; comparing all things she's done)
- The ***most popular event*** of ***all*** is the ***concert*** on Saturday night.
  (superlative form – most important; comparing all the events)

6h.   **NEVER** use *–er* with ***more***. **NEVER** use *–est* with ***most.***

Incorrect	It is the ***most scariest*** ride in the amusement park.
Correct	It is the ***scariest*** ride in the amusement park.
Incorrect	The critics say this movie is ***more funnier*** than that one.
Correct	The critics say this movie is ***funnier*** than that one.

Irregular Comparative and Superlative Forms of Adjectives

6i. Some *comparative* and *superlative forms* are *irregular*. They *do not use –er, -est, more,* or *most* with the *adjective* when *comparing*. They form *new words*.

Adjective	Comparative Form	Superlative Form
good	better	best
bad	worse	worst
little	less	least
much	more	most

- He is a *little* bothered by the statement. *(Adjective)*
- Out of the *two*, he is *less* bothered by the statement. *(Comparative)*
- He is the *least* bothered of *all* the *people* who heard it. *(Superlative)*

Incorrect	*Amy's offer* was the *best* of the *two.*
Correct	*Amy's offer* was the *better* of the *two.* *(comparative form – better; comparing two)*
Incorrect	Looking at *both* situations, his is the *worst.*
Correct	Looking at *both* situations, his is the *worse.* *(comparative form – worse; comparing two)*

Unforgettable Tips!

- Remember! There are *two letters* in *–er*, so use it when *comparing* only *two*. There are *three letters* in *–est*, so use it when *comparing three* or *more*.

  - During the meeting, *Victor* was definitely *calm<u>er</u>* than *Joe*. *(comparing two)*
  - During the meeting, *Kevin* was the *calm<u>est</u>* of the *ten associates*. *(comparing ten)*

- **GOOD! BETTER! BEST! Never take a rest, until *Good* becomes *Better,* and *Better* becomes *Best!*** Think about it like this. *Good* is the *first* level (*adjective – talking about only one*). *Better* is the *second* level (*comparative form of the adjective – comparing two*). *Best* is the *third* level (*superlative form of the adjective – comparing three or more*).

  - This is a *good* product. *(Adjective – one)*
  - The *first product* is *better* than the *second one*. *(Comparative – two)*
  - *This* is the *best product* of the *three*. *(Superlative – three)*

- **NEVER SAY . . .**

more better	**gooder**
badder	**worser**

  Incorrect This is *more better* than that one.
  Correct This is *better* than that one.

Incorrect	We were told that this highway is **gooder** than the other one.
Correct	We were told that this highway is **better** than the other one.
Incorrect	I feel lousy. My cold is **badder** today than it was yesterday.
Correct	I feel lousy. My cold is **worse** today than it was yesterday.
Incorrect	These seats are **worser** than I thought they would be.
Correct	These seats are **worse** than I thought they would be.

Try It Yourself!

Choose the correct word to complete each sentence.

1. She is the (wisest, most wisest) scientist I have met.
2. It was the (cheaper, cheapest) price I could find in the five stores.
3. Out of the two films, this one is (more likely, most likely) to win the award.
4. It is (better, best) that he leaves instead of staying and suffering.
5. The (noisier, noisiest) crowd of the two made a difference in the score.
6. Joseph has the (baddest, worst) attitude of all the young men.

Answers **Please refer back to the rules in (parentheses) to remind you of the explanations in "Chapter 6."**

1. wisest (6e)
2. cheapest (6e)
3. more likely (6f)
4. better (6i)
5. noisier (6d)
6. worst (6i)

7

ADVERBS

❖ **An *adverb* is a word used to *modify or describe a verb*, an *adjective*, or *another adverb*. Adverbs, like *adjectives*, can *add flavor*, *excitement* and *clarity* to your *speaking* and *writing*.**

7a.   Some *adverbs modify verbs*.

- She *spoke admirably* about the president of the organization.
  (*adverb – admirably; verb being modified – spoke.*)
- I do not think he *carefully considered* his options.
  (*adverb – carefully; verb being modified – considered*)

7b.   Some *adverbs modify adjectives*.

- Daniel was *unusually angry* about the arrangements she made.
  (*adverb – unusually; adjective being modified – angry.*)
- Tyson is *absolutely unable* to make a choice right now.
  (*adverb – absolutely; adjective being modified – unable*)

7c.   Some *adverbs modify* other *adverbs*.

- The secretary was *really highly* qualified for the promotion.
  (*adverb – really*; *adverb being modified – highly.*)
- That town *nearly always* receives extra funds for its seniors.
  (*adverb – nearly*; *adverb being modified – always*)

What Do Adverbs Tell About Words They Modify?

7d.   *Adverbs* tell *how, when, where,* or *to what extent* (*how long or how much*) about the words they modify.

- The leading actress *graciously accepted* the applause from the audience.
  (***Graciously* tells *how* the actress accepted the applause.**)
- Because of my prior commitment, I have to *finish* the assignment *later*.
  (***Later* tells *when* I have to finish.**)
- He was *sleeping downstairs* when he heard the loud noise.
  (***Downstairs* tells *where* he was sleeping.**)
- Anita is *completely devoted* to her friends.
  (***Completely* tells *to what extent* Anita is a devoted friend.**)

Adverbs Not Ending in –ly

7e.   *Adverbs* are *easily recognized* because most of
      them *end* in *–ly*. Here is a list of the *most*
      commonly used *adverbs* that do *not end* in *–ly*:

very	almost	well
too	often	already
now	up	far
here	down	then
there	later	near

- Martin *did well* on the entrance exam.
  (*adverb – well; verb being modified – did*)
- I *almost gave* up when I saw how they were
  handling the process.
  (*adverb – almost; verb being modified –*
  gave)
- We had a *very* difficult workout at the gym.
  (*adverb – very; adjective being modified –*
  difficult)
- The house is *too cold*.
  (*adverb – too; adjective being modified –*
  cold)

Using Adverbs and Adjectives

7f.   Most *adverbs* are formed by *adding –ly* to
      adjectives.

Adjectives	*Adverbs*
careful	carefully
sudden	suddenly
confident	confidently

- Anthony is a *confident* young man. *(Adjective)*
- He *confidently* walked up to Mr. Smith and asked for a job. *(Adverb)*
- The car made a *sudden* stop to avoid a terrible accident. *(Adjective)*
- The car *suddenly* stopped to avoid a terrible accident. *(Adverb)*

7g.   To *decide* whether to use an *adjective* or *adverb*, **ask** yourself: **"What word is being modified?"** If a *noun* or *pronoun* is being modified, *use* an *adjective*. If a *verb*, *adjective,* or another *adverb* is being modified, *use* an *adverb*.

- The mayor *spoke* (brief, briefly) about the city's budget.
  What word is being modified? The **verb** *spoke* is being *modified.*
  The mayor spoke briefly about the city's budget.
- David took (careful, carefully) *measures* to protect himself.
  What word is being modified? The **noun** *measures* is being *modified.*
  David took careful measures to protect himself.

Making Comparisons with Adverbs

❖ *Adverbs*, like *adjectives*, use the *comparative form* when comparing *two* persons, places, or things. Use the *superlative form* when comparing *three* or *more.*

7h. Add *–er* to some *adverbs* when using the *comparative* form.

- *Dave* arrived *earlier* than *Sheila* did. *(adverb – earlier; modifying the verb arrived; comparing Dave and Sheila)*
- They *screamed louder* for *him* than for *Eric.* *(adverb – louder; modifying the verb screamed; comparing him and Eric)*

7i. Add *–est* to some *adverbs* when using the *superlative* form.

- Of the *three* of them, James arrived the *earliest.* *(adverb – earliest; modifying the verb arrived; comparing three)*
- Out of all the runners, they *screamed loudest* for *Dan.* *(adverb – loudest; modifying the verb screamed; comparing all the runners)*

7j. When *comparing two persons, places,* or *things* with *adverbs* that *end* with *–ly,* put *more before* the *adverbs.*

- The *first restaurant* is *more highly* recommended than the *second one.* *(adverb – more highly; modifying the verb recommended; comparing first restaurant and the second one)*
- The *seminar last week* was *more professionally* presented than *this one.* *(adverb – more professionally; modifying the verb presented; comparing seminar last week and this one)*

7k.   When comparing *three* or *more persons, places,* or *things* with *adverbs ending* in *–ly,* use *most* with the adverb.

- The *first restaurant* was the *most highly* recommended of *all* the *restaurants* in the area. *(adverb – most highly; modifying the verb recommended; comparing all the restaurants)*
- The *seminar last week* was the *most professionally presented* of the *six* that I attended. *(adverb – most professionally; modifying the verb presented; comparing the six seminars)*

Using Good and Well; Bad and Badly

Knowing when to use *good* and *well*, as well as *bad* and *badly,* is often *confusing*.

7l.   *Good* and *bad* are *adjectives* that tell *what kind* and *modify nouns* and *pronouns*.

- The *orchestra* was really *good.*
  (adjective – good; noun – orchestra; tells what kind of orchestra)
- Jeff presented a *good point* to the council.
  (adjective – good; noun – point; tells what kind of point)
- That was *bad advice* that she gave to her partner.
  (adjective – bad; noun – advice; tells what kind of advice)
- The report has a *bad section* that needs to be done again.
  (adjective – bad; noun – section; tells what kind of section)

7m. The words *well* and *badly* are *adverbs* that tell *how something is done,* and they *modify verbs.*

- The orchestra *played well.*
  (adverb – well; verb – played; tells how the orchestra played)
- Jeff's point *was well presented* to the council.
  (adverb – well; verb – was presented; tells how the point was presented)
- That advice *was badly given* to her partner.
  (adverb – well; verb – was given; tells how the advice was given)
- The report has a section that *is badly done.*
  (adverb – badly; verb – is done; tells how the section was done)

A Closer Look . . .

Good or Well

7n.   When speaking about someone's *emotional health*, use the *adjective good*.

- Larry is not *good* today. He's *upset* about something.
  (adjective – good; emotional health – upset)
- I don't feel *good* about what I did. I have *made* a *terrible decision*.
  (adjective – good; emotional health – made a terrible decision)

7o.   Even though *well* is an *adverb*, it can *also* be used as an *adjective* when it means *healthy.*

- *Larry* is *well* today.
  (adjective – well; means - Larry is healthy.)
- Since *I* wasn't *well,* I cancelled my plans.
  (adjective – well; means – I wasn't healthy.)

Unforgettable Tips!

☛ *Never* use *more* and *better together*.

Incorrect	This television show is *more better* than that one.
Correct	This television show is *better* than that one.
Incorrect	It would be *more better* if you arrived before your guests.
Correct	It would be *better* if you arrived before your guests.

☛ *In Chapter 5 – Prepositions, Rule 5f says: Avoid using a preposition at the end of a sentence.* Sometimes it may seem as if a sentence is ending with a preposition, but it is not. *Some prepositions* are *also adverbs*. If is an *adverb*, the word can be used *alone* at the *end* of the sentence. If it *comes at the beginning of a prepositional phrase*, it is a *preposition* and *must have* an *object* of the preposition *following* it.

- I had to *drive around.*
  (adverb – around; modifying the verb drive)
- I had to drive *around the block.*
  (preposition – around; introduces the prepositional phrase "around the parking lot"; object of the preposition – block)

☛ It is the *Good vs. Well Attack!*

After a week in bed with the *flu,* I woke up and said, **"Finally, I feel well today, and I am ready for a great day."** That soon changed. I dealt with one problem after another. By the end of the morning, I was saying, **"I don't feel so good now. I just want to scream!"**

- Let's examine the above statements:

  - *Well* was used in the *beginning* because I had been sick for a week, and finally, *I don't feel sick* any more. *I feel well.*
    (adjective – well; modifying the pronoun I; talking about my physical health – I am healthy.)

  - *Good* was used at the *end* because the *problems aggravated me: I don't feel good. I want to scream.*
    (adjective – good; modifying I; talking about my emotional health – I am upset.)

- ALWAYS remember . . .

  - *Well – Physical Health . . . Body!*
  - *Good – Emotional Health . . . Mind and Emotions!*

Try It Yourself!

A. Which word is being modified by the underlined adverb? Tell if it is an adjective, verb, or adverb.

1. We **boldly** walked into the crowd.
2. Sam made the same mistake **too** often.
3. There are **totally** serious consequences for the previous actions.

B. Choose the correct word to complete each sentence.

1. The lounge on the upper level is (more gorgeously, most gorgeously) decorated than the one on the lower level.
2. Their friend performed (bad, badly).
3. That is a (real, really) good look for you.
4. Margaret did (good, well) on the entrance exam.
5. I don't feel (good, well) about this conversation.
6. Stacey's family (cheerful, cheerfully) supported her cause.

Answers   **Please refer back to the rules in (parentheses) to remind you of the explanations in "Chapter 7."**

A. 1.   walked; verb (7a)
    2.   often; adverb (7c)
    3.   serious; adjective (7b)

B. 1.   more gorgeously (7j)
    2.   badly (7g, 7m)
    3.   Really (7g)
    4.   well (7m)
    5.   good (7n)
    6.   cheerfully (7a)

DOUBLE NEGATIVES

❖ **A *negative* is a word that says "*No.*" Double negatives are *two negative words* used in the *same* sentence. *Avoid* using *double negatives* in both your speaking and your writing.**

8a.   The most ***common negative words*** are:

no	nothing	never
no one	no more	nowhere
not	nobody	none

- There is ***nothing*** wrong with this apartment. *(one negative word – nothing)*
- I hope you ***never*** change your great attitude. *(one negative word – never)*
- ***Nobody*** told me that we had to be there. *(one negative word – Nobody)*

8b.   Be very ***careful*** with the ***negative word*** "**not.**" It is often used as ***part*** of a ***contraction***. The ***contraction also*** becomes a ***negative word.***

have + not = haven't   is + not = isn't
are + not = aren't   do + not = don't
was + not = wasn't   did + not = didn't

- ***Wasn't*** that your suggestion he gave them? *(one negative word – Wasn't)*

- The products I ordered two weeks ago *haven't* arrived yet.
  (one negative word – haven't)
- The homeowners *aren't* impressed with the new amenities.
  (one negative word – aren't)

8c.   When *two negative words* are used in a sentence, a *double negative* is formed.

- There is *no one nowhere* in this deserted building. *(Incorrect)*
  (double negatives – no one, nowhere)
- *Never* allow *nothing* to keep you from doing your best. *(Incorrect)*
  (double negatives – Never, nothing)
- She *wasn't* spending *no more* time on that subject. *(Incorrect)*
  (double negatives – wasn't, no more)

8d.   Some common *positive words* are:

any	**ever**	**someone**
anyone	**everybody**	**something**
any more	**everyone**	**somewhere**
anywhere	**everywhere**	

- *Everyone* has finally voted.
  (one positive word – Everyone)
- I am allergic to *something* the chef used in that dish.
  (one positive word – something)
- The wedding planner can't find *anywhere* to have the bridal shower.
  (one positive word – anywhere)

8e.   Sometimes we *need* to use a *positive word* to *avoid* having *two negative words* in the same *sentence.*

- I *never* received *any* of their donations. *(negative word – never; positive word – any)*
- There is *nothing* left for *anyone* to do. *(negative word – nothing; positive word – anyone)*
- *Don't* put *someone* in the position who can't handle it. *(negative word – Don't; positive word – someone)*

Incorrect	*No one* did *nothing* to help her. *(two negatives – Nobody, no one)*
Correct	*No one* did *anything* to help her. *(negative – No one; positive – anything)*
Incorrect	*None* of this *shouldn't* make a difference. *(two negatives – None, shouldn't)*
Correct	*None* of this *should* make a difference. *(negative – None; positive – should)*
Incorrect	*Nobody never* attends the after-work parties. *(two negatives – Nobody, never)*
Correct	*Nobody ever* attends the after-work parties. *(negative – Nobody; positive – ever)*

*Removing not (n't) from the contraction makes the verb a positive, so it can be used with a negative word.

Unforgettable Tips!

☛ One of the most famous *commercial jingles* was, *"Nobody doesn't like Sara Lee."* The *advertisers* of the product definitely *didn't want* anyone to *think* that the *product wasn't good.* They *wanted people* to *buy* it. Then, *why say that?* They obviously *knew* something *about double negatives.* What they *really* were *saying* about their *product* was that it was so *good*, and *"Everybody does like Sara Lee."*

☛ *Sometimes* when we use a *double negative* in our speaking or writing, we are actually *saying* that the *opposite* of the statement is *true*.

> **"I don't never want to see you again!"**
> Are you sure? Do you really mean that?
> How are you truly feeling? **"I do want to see you again, BUT I'm upset right now."**
> **You know . . .!!!!**

Try It Yourself!

A. Tell if each sentence is correct or incorrect.

1. We haven't seen nobody since we returned from our vacation.
2. The renovated building has nothing to assist the handicap tenants.
3. I don't never want to have to choose between the two of you.
4. We found out that the patient wasn't nowhere on that floor.

B. Choose the correct word to complete each sentence.

1. She didn't do (nothing, anything) wrong to receive that treatment from them.
2. The boss never asked (none of us, any of us) to do (nothing, something) unreasonable.
3. I want absolutely (nothing, anything) to do with that situation.
4. Didn't (nobody, anybody) foresee the problem?
5. After the huge loss, a fan could be found (nowhere, anywhere) in the parking lot.
6. Nobody (didn't, did) the proper screening of the applicants.
7. I won't (never, ever) waste your valuable time.

Answers Please refer back to the rules in (parentheses) to remind you of the explanations in "Chapter 8."

A. 1. Incorrect (8b, 8c)
   2. Correct (8a)
   3. Incorrect (8b, 8c)
   4. Incorrect (8b, 8c)

B. 1. anything (8e)
   2. any of us; something (8e)
   3. nothing (8a)
   4. anybody (8e)
   5. nowhere (8a)
   6. did (8e)
   7. ever (8e)

INDEX

Adjectives, 101-114
   after nouns, 102; before nouns, 101; definition of, 101; kinds of,
   101
Adjective or Pronoun, 103-104
Articles – *the, a,* and *an,* 105
   An before vowels and vowel sounds, 105
Comparing with *More* and *Most,* 110
   comparative form – *more* before the adjective, 110; *-er* – NEVER
   with *more,* 111; -est, NEVER with *most,* 111; superlative form –
   most before the adjective, 110-111
Demonstrative Adjectives – *This, That, These,* and *Those,* 102-
103
   these and *those* with plural nouns, 102; *this* and *that* with
   singular nouns, 102; with *kind* and *sort,* 103; with *kinds* and
   sorts, 103
Irregular Comparative and Superlative Forms of
Adjectives, 112
Making Comparisons with Adjectives, 109-104
   comparative form with *–er, 109;* superlative form with
   -est, 109-110
Special Adjectives, 104
   capital letters, 104; proper adjectives and special
   endings, 104-105

Adverbs, 115-122
   definition of, 115; modifying verbs, 115; modifying
   adjectives, 115; modifying adverbs, 116
Adverbs and Adjectives, 117-118
   adding *–ly* to adjectives, 117-118; using adjective or
   adverb, 118
Adverbs Not Ending *-ly,* 117
Adverbs Tell About Words They Modify, 116
Good or Well, 112

adjective – *good,* 122; adverb *well* as an adjective, 122
Making Comparisons with Adverbs, 119-120
    comparative form with *–er,* 119; ; *more* before the
    adverb, 119-120; *most* before the adverb, 120;
    superlative form with *–est,* 129
Using Good and Well; Bad and Badly, 120-121
    adjectives – *good* and *bad,* 120-121; adverbs – *well* and
    badly, 121

Double Negatives, 127-131
    avoiding double negatives, 129; common negative
    words, 127; common positive words, 127

Nouns, 7-17
    definition of, 7; common nouns, 7; plural nouns 7-9; proper
    nouns,7; singular nouns, 7-9
Forming the Plural of Nouns, 7-9
    adding *–es,* 7-8; adding *–s,* 7; changing *–y* to *–i* adding *–es,* 8;
    nouns ending with *–f* and *–fe,* 8; nouns – the same in singular and
    plural, 9; plural without adding *–s* or *–es,* 8-9
Plural Possessive Nouns, 11
    apostrophe and *–s* with days of the week and months of the year,
    14; apostrophe with person's name ending with an *–s,* 15-16;
    apostrophe and *–s* with plural nouns not ending in *–s,* 12; plural
    noun or plural possessive, 12-13; using an apostrophe after an
    –s, 11-12
Possessive Nouns, 11-16
    definition of, 11
Singular Possessive Nouns, 11
    using an apostrophe before an *–s,* 11

Parts of Speech, 5-6

Prepositions, 91-99

definition of, 91; commonly used prepositions, 91

Prepositional Phrases, 93-94

definition of, 93; object pronouns after prepositions, 93-94; with more than one object, 93

Prepositions *Between* and *Among*, 95

difference between, 95-96

Prepositions at the End of Sentences, 96-97

Subject/Verb Agreement and the Object of the Preposition, 94

singular subject – -*s* on verb; plural subject – basic form of verb, 94; verb agreeing with the subject, not the object, 94; subject never in preposition, 94

Pronouns, 43-68

antecedents with pronouns, 43; definition of, 43

Indefinite Pronouns, 65-66

plural indefinite pronouns, 66; singular indefinite pronouns, 65

Object Pronouns, 53-54, 57

after action verbs, 53; after prepositions, 53-54; list of, 53

Plural pronouns, 43, 45

joined by conjunction *and*, 44; list of, 45

Possessive Pronouns, 63-65

before nouns, 63; stand alone, 63-64; with gerunds (nouns, instead of verbs, ending with –ing), 64

Possessive Pronouns and Contractions, 65

its and it's, 65; their and they're, 65; your and you're, 65

Pronouns After Than and As, 55

object pronoun after, 55; subject pronoun after, 55

Pronouns and Antecedents in Special Ways, 44

Reflexive Pronouns, 56

ending with, -self, 56

Relative Pronouns, 59

Who and Whom, 59-62; Whoever and Whomever, 60

Singular Pronouns, 44

joined by conjunctions *or, either-or, neither-nor, 44;* list of, 44

Subject Pronouns, 49-50, 57

after state-of-being verbs, 49-50; before action verbs, 49; followed by a noun, 50; list of, 49

Subject and Verb Agreement, 69-99

adding and –s to the verb, 69; plural nouns and pronouns as subjects, 69-70; plural subject not ending with an –s, 71 pronouns *I* and *you* as subjects, 70; singular nouns and a pronouns as subjects, 69; singular noun ending with an –s, 70-71

Compound Subjects with *or, either-or,* and *neither-nor,* 80
adding –s to the verb with singular nouns and pronouns, 80; basic form of the verb with plural nouns and pronouns, 80-81; both a singular and plural subject, agree with word closer to verb, 81

Conjunction *and* in a compound subject, 76
are and *were* with *and* in the compound subject, 78; joined as a singular subject with *and,* 78-79; plural compound subjects; connected with the conjunction *and,* 78; plural subject, not contraction, 86; same rules for singular subject and verb, 86; singular indefinite pronouns joined by *and,* 79; with *or, either-or, neither-nor,* 87

Does and *Do* with Singular and Plural Subjects, 73 -74

Has and *Have* with Singular and Plural Subjects, 73
do with plural subjects, 74; *has* with singular subjects, 73; *have* with plural subjects, 73; pronouns *you* and *I* with have, 73; pronouns *you* and *I* with plural subjects, 74

Here, There, and *Where* with Contractions, 86

Is, Are, Was, and *Were* with Singular and Plural Subjects, 72
plural subjects with *are* or *were,* 72; pronoun *I* with *am* or *was,* 72; pronoun *you* with *are* or *were, 72;* singular subject with *is* or was, 72

Subject and Verb Agreement with a Compound Subject, 76-87

Subject and Verb Agreement with *Here, There,* and *Where,* 84-87
plural subjects with plural verbs, 84-85; singular subjects with singular verbs, 84

Were in the Subjunctive Mood, 74-75

Verbs, 19-42

definition of, 29

Action Verbs, 19, 49, 53

Confusing Verbs, 35-37
bought and *brought,* 36-37, 40; *can* and *may,* 35-46, 40-41; *insure* and *ensure,* 37; *lie* and *lay,* 36; *sit* and *set,* 35

Future Tense of Verbs, 29
helping verbs *will* and *shall,* 29

Helping Verbs, 21-22
common helping verbs, 21; main verbs, 21-22; main verbs ending

with *–ing,* 22
Irregular verbs in the past tense, 27-29
  helping verbs with past participle, 28; same in the past tense and
  past participle, 28-29
Past Tense of Verbs, 25-26
  adding *–ed* to the basic form, 26
Present Tense of Verbs, 25
  adding *–s* and *–es* with a singular noun or pronoun, 25; basic form
  of the verb with plural verbs and pronouns *I* and *you,* 25; dropping
  the *–e* before adding *–ed,* 26-27; state-of-being verb *are* with
  plural nouns, 25; past participle, 26; state-of-being verb *is* with a
  singular subject, 25-26
Principal Parts of Common Irregular Verbs, 31-32
  common irregular verbs with the past participle, 31-32; helping
  verbs before the past participle, 31
State-of-being verbs, 20, 25, 49-50
  linking verbs, 20
Staying in the same verb tense, 29-30
Verbs Confused with Words Are Not Verbs, 38
  accept and *except,* 38-39; *affect* and *effect,* 38; *lost* and *loss,* 39,
Verb Tenses, 25
  definition of, 25

Unforgettable Tips

- *Apostrophe* or *Apostrophe* and *–s* on a *person's name ending*
  with an *–s,* 15
- *Bought* and *Brought,* 40
- *Can* and *May,* 40-41
- *Compound Object Pronouns* After Preposition and Action
  Verbs, 57
- *Compound Subjects* as *Singular Subjects,* 82
- *Confusion* with *Prepositional Phrases,* 98
- Conjunction *Or with Singular and Plural Subjects,* 82
- *Difference* between *"a"* and *"and"* Correctly, 106-107
- *Double Negatives,* 130
- *Good vs. Well Attack,* 123-124
- *Happy New Year,* 15
- *Here, There,* and *Where,* 88
- *Irregular Past Participle* – Never alone, 33
- *Lost* and *Loss,* 41

- My *Valentine,* 15
- *Men's* and *Women's* with an Apostrophe, 15
- *Never* put an *–s* on *Sheep.* 10
- *Never* put an *–s* on the *verb* if the subject is *I.* 76-77
- *Never use* **contractions** *as a* **possessive pronoun.** 67
- *Never* use **here** *or* **there** with **this, that, these,** and **those.** 106
- *Never* use *is* or *was* with *you* or *they.* 76
- *Never* use **more** and **better together.** 123
- *Never* use the pronoun **them before** a **noun.** 106
- *No –s* at the End of the Pronoun *Mine,* 67
- *No –s* on *Subject - -s* on the *Verb,* 76
- *One-word* Sentences, 23
- *Possessive Pronouns* before a *Gerund (noun* ending in *– ing),* 68
- *Present, Past,* and *Future Tenses,* 33
- *Preposition* or *Adverb,* 123
- *Pronouns* Before Nouns, 51
- *-s* on *Subject – No –s* on the *Verb,* 76
- *Subject Pronoun* After State-of-Being Verbs, 51
- *Subject Pronouns* and *Object Pronouns Don't Mix,* 57
- Using *–er* and *–est* on *Adjectives,* 113
- *Verbs* ending in *–ing,* 23
- *Who* and *Whom* in a *Question,* 61-62

ABOUT THE AUTHOR

Valerie Payton is a literacy coach, consultant, editor, and author. Her latest project is *DON'T SAY THAT,* a communication book that bridges the gap of the *spoken words* and *written words* of the English Language. She believes that the proper use of language, combined with the power of understanding the importance of effective communication, can transform lives, communities, and the nation. She is a literacy advocate, determined to make a difference.

Valerie is an adjunct professor at The City University of New York – Borough of Manhattan Community College (BMCC), where she teaches Academic & Critical Reading (ACR) Courses in the Freshman Summer Immersion Program. She prepares the students for success in mastering a full range of college-level courses that require critical reading and comprehension, as well as intense vocabulary and writing skills.

With over thirty (30) years of service in the Department of Education of the City of New York as a teacher, literacy coach, consultant, and playwright, Valerie has impacted the lives of students, staff, administrators, and parents. She is a workshop facilitator, curriculum writer and developer, a test-taking strategies' specialist, and a sought-after seminar presenter. Her sessions are met with digestible content and delivered in ways that make them easy to implement long after the event is over.

Valerie has been recognized as District 5's "Renaissance

Teacher of the Year" at P.S. 133/The Fred R. Moore School in Harlem. She also received recognition in the 2000, 2002, 2004, and 2006 editions of *Who's Who Among America's Teachers* – an accomplishment that puts her in the one percent of elementary school educators with multiple inclusions, since the publications honor teachers that inspired and made a significant difference in the lives of the nation's highest-performing high school students. Under the leadership of Jim Carroll of Syracuse University in New York, Valerie, along with thirty (30) other New York City teachers, was chosen to participate in a Talented and Gifted Honors Project. They wrote a special curriculum (Project LEGAL/Project CRITICAL) to enhance students' problem-solving and critical thinking skills, using law-related materials. School districts adopted the program.

As a freelance editor, she has worked on several writing projects. She was afforded the honor of editing a movie script and a documentary for Hollywood's Writer and Producer Ronald Lang . . . *All About the Benjamins (2002)*.

Valerie has a Bachelor of Arts Degree in English Language Arts from Hunter College in New York City. She was awarded a Master of Education (M.Ed.) in Reading from Antioch College in Yellow Springs, Ohio. She was trained in the "Teachers College Reading and Writing Project" under the tutelage of Lucy Calkins and her team at Columbia University in New York. She also studied and collaborated with Susan Radley Brown, a nationally recognized literacy consultant and founder of the "Accelerated Literacy Learning Program" (A.L.L), and her curriculum development team.

Valerie currently resides in New Jersey. She enjoys giving "ordinary people" the confidence to pursue extraordinary dreams . . . empowering them to become "The Masters of Their Communication."

CORRECT RESPONSES TO SENTENCES ON THE BACK COVER

There is only ONE CORRECT SENTENCE. Can you believe it? Get ready to explore *DON'T SAY THAT* and find out why. Discover the rules, explanations, and "Unforgettable Tips" that will enlighten, inspire, encourage, and even challenge you to sharpen and perfect your communication skills. Stop wondering: "Did I say that right?" As you unlock the mystery, become *The Master of Your Communication.*

1. He will work diligently with you and **me** to finish the project.
   (Chapter 3 – "Using Compound Object Pronouns after the Preposition")
2. There isn't **anything** we can do to change the outcome. There **is** nothing we can do to change the outcome.
   (Chapter 8 – "Double Negatives")
3. You made a **really** good decision about your future.
   (Chapter 7 – "Some Adverbs Modify Adjectives"; "Using Adverbs and Adjectives")
4. All the **players'** statistics show that they are true champions.
   (Chapter 1 – "Plural Possessive Nouns")
5. Neither Mary nor Barbara **understands** Larry's point of view.
   (Chapter 4 – "Using Compound Subjects with Or, Either-or, and Neither-nor")
6. THIS IS THE **ONLY CORRECT SENTENCE!**
   (Chapter 5 – "Subject/Verb Agreement and the Object of the Preposition")
7. **Doesn't** it seem strange that no one knew about this?
   (Chapter 4 – "Using Does and Do with Singular and Plural Subjects")
8. When I look at both articles, I think the first one is the **better** choice.
   (Chapter 6 – "Irregular Comparative and Superlative Forms of Adjectives")
9. **Whom** should I see about setting up an interview?
   (Chapter 3 – "Using the Relative Pronouns Who and Whom")
10. That movie was so good! I **saw** it three times. I **have seen** it three times. **I've seen** it three times.
    (Chapter 2 – "Irregular Verbs in the Past Tense/Principal Parts of Common Irregular Verbs/Using the Past Participle Correctly")

Congratulations!
You Are

THE MASTER

OF *Your*

COMMUNICATION

DON'T *Say* THAT

Made in the USA
Charleston, SC
27 February 2015